MORE PRAISE FOR
THE AUTHEN

The Authentic Brand gets to the he___ ___ _____ _____es connect with their customers by sp___ng to them at their level, never talking down to them. It's smart business and marketing for today's smart consumer culture.

> **Jerry Greenfield**—*Co-Founder Ben & Jerry's Homemade*

NOW is the time to grab market share and Christopher Rosica's book provides practical approaches for making this happen.

> **Verne Harnish**—*Author of* Mastering the Rockefeller Habits *and Founder of the Entrepreneurs' Organization (EO)*

A wonderful, increasingly enjoyable book. I would recommend it to anyone who loves to be challenged, and even more to anyone who isn't ready for it.

> **Michael E. Gerber**—*Author of* The E-Myth Books

Stonyfield Farm is a "word of mouth" brand, our success built one cup of yogurt at a time. In our experience, brand loyalty comes from paying attention to what our consumers care about: healthy food, healthy people, and a healthy planet. *The Authentic Brand* helps readers learn the importance of speaking to customers' intelligence and creating an authentic partnership between company and consumer.

> **Gary Hirshberg**—*CE-Yo, Stonyfield Farm*

Rosica's book is dead on. He has captured the essence of how to create brand equity and awareness for a successful business. This book provides outstanding insight from an A-list of people who have built enormously successful companies. If you're building a brand for your business, this is a must read.

Brien Biondi—*Executive Director, Chief Executives Organization (CEO), Former CEO of Young Entrepreneurs' Organization (YEO)*

Christopher Rosica offers fresh insights into the unspoken emotional needs of the customer. This book shows how taking the time to build a truly authentic brand can deliver lifelong customers and robust profits.

Geoff Smart, Ph.D.—*Chairman and CEO, ghSMART, Topgrading Co-Author and Master Trainer*

Far too many entrepreneurs struggle with marketing their businesses effectively. Rosica's timely release has made the complex idea of branding simple to understand and execute. I recommend this as an essential read for all successful entrepreneurs.

Vijay K. Tirathrai—*Past International President, Young Entrepreneurs' Organization, Founder and Managing Director, Fabulous Target*

THE Authentic Brand

How Today's Top Entrepreneurs Connect With Customers

by Christopher Rosica

Featuring the Priceless Insights of:
Wally "Famous" Amos
Jerry Baldwin, *Co-Founder, Starbucks, Principal, Peet's Coffee*
Bobbi Brown, *Bobbi Brown Cosmetics*
Ben Cohen, *Ben & Jerry's Homemade*
Jerry Greenfield, *Ben & Jerry's Homemade*
Gary Hirshberg, *Stonyfield Farm*
Jim Koch, *Samuel Adams Beer*
David Neeleman, *JetBlue Airways*
David Oreck, *Oreck Corporation*
Roxanne Quimby, *Burt's Bees*
Andy and Kate Spade, *Kate Spade*
Jeff Taylor, *Monster.com*

NOBLE PRESS

Published by Noble Press

Noble Press, 641 Lexington Avenue, 14th floor, New York, NY 10022, U.S.A.

Second Printing

Copies of this book may be purchased at:
www.TheAuthenticBrand.com
Telephone: 866-843-5600

ISBN 978-0-9793101-1-9

Printed in the United States of America

To my family—
Wendy, Natalie, and Cole.

Also to my mom and dad, co-workers, and clients,
whom I admire and appreciate.

Final thanks to EO, YPO, CEO, WPO, and
similar organizations that support and
promote entrepreneurship.

TABLE OF CONTENTS

Authenticity   I

CHAPTER 1:
Facing the Truth: There Are Too Many "Faceless" Companies   1

CHAPTER 2:
Doing Good to Do Well: How Cause-Related Marketing
Builds Brands and Good Will   23

CHAPTER 3:
Speak to Your Customers' Intelligence   47

CHAPTER 4:
"Geo-Branding"   57

CHAPTER 5:
Story-Telling Creates Even Bigger Brands   65

CHAPTER 6:
Flying Under the Radar: A Great Way to Crash and Burn   75

TABLE OF CONTENTS

CHAPTER 7:
Leadership Qualities and Beliefs   87

    Leadership Styles   88

    Time Management   95

    Influences and Role Models   99

    Finding and Retaining Talented People   108

    Managing Conflict   124

    Accountability, Measuring Results, and Goal Setting   125

    Too Many Meetings?   132

    Showing Vulnerability   133

    Family and Belief Systems   137

    Confronting Failure   143

    Mentoring   150

CHAPTER 8:
Shared Insights and Experiences   155

    Is There a Better Mousetrap?   155

    Mission Statements   169

    Can You Take the Business Too Seriously?   175

    The Importance of Education   178

    Business Tools   185

    Sharing Equity and Taking on Partners   190

    Creating an Exit Strategy   194

    Letting Go   198

    Macro-Managing—Not Micro-Managing   204

    Leaving a Legacy   208

    Final Thoughts   211

Authenticity

"We don't try to pretend we are something we're not," Gary Hirshberg, President and CE-Yo of Stonyfield Farm, said when I asked him how he connects with his customers. "You just have to allow yourself to follow your instincts and not live in fear of the consumer, but *respect* the consumer's judgment. You have to trust that, if you are telling them sensible things and dealing with them on their level, they will respect you."

How do you actually *connect* with your customers?

The answer is "with authenticity."

This book is about how today's top entrepreneurs connect to their customers with authenticity.

"We can ship our yogurt 3,000 miles," Hirshberg told me. "But it's the last 18 inches that make all the difference—getting that spoon to the customer's mouth!"

How does Stonyfield Farm move its product that last 18 inches? And, once they do, what is it that creates devoted brand-fans? Authenticity.

Most, if not all books, while being written, take on a life of their own. Often, they evolve into something more than what the author originally intended. When I started this book, I assumed that, when interviewing a dozen or so renowned entrepreneurs, I would find many unambiguous leadership traits and practices. However, I soon discovered that these people had disparate styles and approaches. While each of these entrepreneurs has created a prominent, even iconic, brand, the way they led their companies was exceptionally diverse. The one overarching theme that I did discover when talking with these gifted entrepreneurs was *authenticity*. Each of them created substantial companies based upon meaningful missions, hence the title—and common theme—of this book.

In accordance with some of the definitions found for the word "authentic," the one referred to here is: *worthy of belief and trust, and neither false nor unoriginal*—in short, *genuine* and *original*.

Authenticity produces connectivity with highly satisfied customers through touching people at an *emotional* level, driven by such product or corporate traits as unparalleled quality, commitment to customer service, true concern for the community, charitable involvement, and the remarkable business cultures these entrepreneurs have created.

Moreover, I discovered several common themes in their marketing methodologies, which comprise *The Authentic Brand's* first six chapters.

This book was originally conceived while I was enrolled in an intensive course on entrepreneurship at MIT that was suitably named "The Birthing of Giants." The Birthing of Giants is a three-year, MBA-modeled curriculum created by Verne Harnish, founder of the Entrepreneurs' Organization (EO), in conjunction with the MIT Enterprise Forum and *Inc. Magazine.* Each year, the program brings together 60 young entrepreneurs under the age of 40 who are founders or managing partners of companies grossing more than a million dollars in annual revenues. The program was designed to identify and bring together the next generation of entrepreneurial leaders and to provide the blending of practice and theory that is required to succeed in today's business environment.

This gave me an idea for a book in which I would interview several celebrated entrepreneurs and share their secrets to success, including their leadership and marketing insights. I wanted to write a business book based on the *practical and real-life experiences* of successful, self-starting entrepreneurs, rather than academic conjecture or criteria.

As a member of the Entrepreneurs' Organization (formerly known as YEO) since 1999, I have attended dozens of learning events in conjunction with various EO chapters globally, as well as the Young Presidents' and World Presidents' Organizations (YPO and WPO, respectively). During this time, I have benefitted greatly from the learning that occurs from the experiences of others with similar challenges and aspirations. As Douglas Adams, author of *The Hitchhiker's Guide to the Galaxy*, once said, "Human beings, who are almost unique in having the ability to learn from the experience of others, are also remarkable for their apparent disinclination to do so." I cannot say enough about these powerful groups for entrepreneurs and corporate leaders. They harness the power of shared learning through peer-to-peer support and education.

With this in mind, *The Authentic Brand* is designed to give a behind-the-scenes look at a dozen of today's top entrepreneurs to discover their leadership, management, and marketing triumphs and lessons. Furthermore, because of the insights revealed by our interviewees, the take-home value is remarkable and applicable to all types of businesses, regardless of size or industry. After all, leadership and marketing are universal and transcend industry nuances. Each pioneer has risen to the top amid an abundance of competitors.

It is plain, in our contemporary society, that we are constantly inundated with commercial messages. Breaking through this clutter can mean remarkable success for entrepreneurs, business leaders, and managers alike. Our purchasing decisions are influenced by so many factors. These range from packaging (and what it evokes) and the advertising messages we received during our formative years —to the tone and feel of a company's message about its brand. How a brand resonates with its customers is also influenced by positive editorial feature stories generated by public relations and personal recommendations or word-of-mouth, perhaps the two most influential factors. Think about your own purchasing decisions. In the end, sustainability and staying power come down to the ability of the company to keep its brand promise. In short, *authenticity.*

In recent years, consumer-product marketing has changed. Years ago, many companies, particularly the well-known giants, used a mix of print, radio, and television advertising to establish their brand. Today, this model is proving difficult for companies building a new brand from the ground up. Cost of entry, the dilution of media, and the fact that we are bombarded with so many messages limit the feasibility of the earlier model. Beyond that, today's savvy customer expects and demands more than could be provided through the old advertising model. These days, people value and reward companies that provide exceptional quality and service and stand for something beyond profits.

It used to be that people primarily evaluated products on the basis of price, but this has indisputably changed. Only a few of the companies that we've profiled compete on cost. In fact, many charge more than their competitors. The lesson here is that if you build an *authentic* brand, there is no reason a business can't charge $1,200 for a handbag, $750 for a vacuum cleaner, $6 for a one-pound bag of cookies, or $4 for a cup of coffee.

Just as today's consumers choose products and services for the value they offer, they also consider the *values* of the person or the company behind the brand—they are looking for authenticity. Simon Sinek, an intuitive marketing consultant and the founder of Sinek Partners, says, "People are loyal to companies that offer more than just products and their associated benefits. They buy *a lifestyle, purpose, cause, or belief.*" The entrepreneurs featured here have successfully connected at this level, offering genuine and original customer *experiences* — and stand for a lifestyle, cause, or belief system.

All of the business leaders and brand-builders in this book *speak to their customers' intelligence*, and they are about *more than just commerce.* For example, Ben & Jerry have worked actively to make the world a better place. Wally Amos has helped tens of thousands of adults to read. Bobbi Brown donates pallet-loads of products to women in need. Gary Hirshberg brings healthy snack foods into schools and works toward improving the environment. More than price or the superficial elements of the product, each of these brands resonates with the customer. There is a feeling associated with these brands—something real and substantial. It is authenticity.

Today, many successful and popular brands are created *without* an advertising budget. How is this done? How can a company create a dedicated brand following? Can a company be steered strictly by consumer-centric or customer-driven needs? What brand or corporate characteristics command our attention and why—and how does emotion come into play when creating strong customer connectivity? How are "sticky" brands born and sustained? How do an entrepreneur's leadership traits and styles shape the building of a brand? What are some of the key ingredients needed to build brand equity so that, when the business is sold, it demands top dollar—selling for a multiple of revenues that ignores all logical accounting principals or formulas?

I contemplated each of these questions before I spoke with these entrepreneurs. Therefore, this book evolved into an examination of how contrasting, highly successful business leaders have built devoted brand followings through non-traditional marketing and management practices. For these reasons, the marketing intelligence and essentials for creating genuine, sticky brands—found in the words of these entrepreneurs—are priceless.

Each person with whom I spoke when compiling the content of this book has made his/her share of mistakes, and was ready to discuss these openly. Some have been publicly scrutinized, not for their integrity or malicious intentions, but for judgments or decisions they made that backfired. We know from their experiences and countless others that failure is a core commonality and often precedes great success; the word "entrepreneur" indicates risk. *The American Heritage Dictionary* defines an entrepreneur as: *A person who organizes, operates and assumes the risk for a business venture.*

One of the featured entrepreneurs, David Neeleman of JetBlue Airways, went through a major crisis while I was completing this book. However, after interviewing him, I do not doubt his good intentions or competency. Most importantly, I do not doubt his ability to learn from adversity.

In *The Authentic Brand*, I chose to use the experience of these prominent entrepreneurs to provide an excellent motivational tool for aspiring entrepreneurs, seasoned business leaders, and all professionals who are growth-minded and students of the art of business, marketing, and brand-building. We will examine how these business leaders profoundly connect with their customers and:

- Provide a unique marketing advantage
- Shape the brand and identity
- Differentiate the brand from its competition
- Build a loyal customer base
- Create a flavor or flair that would not otherwise be possible
- Maintain consistency and keep the "brand promise"
- Give back a portion of their success to causes about which they feel strongly
- Form a company that establishes widespread awareness
- Generate significant brand equity and corporate value

As you will soon find, the entrepreneurs I had the privilege of interviewing have candidly shared their marketing strategies, their methods for speaking on their customers' level, their leadership lessons, and their experiences. They share their weaknesses as well as their strengths, both of which are undoubtedly valuable. In looking over the shoulders of these entrepreneurs, and in following the evolution of their brands, you will see that each built the brand with a sense of purpose and substance and with a commitment to authenticity.

I'm sure that you will find value in these insights from these accomplished, visionary entrepreneurs.

—Christopher Rosica
Paramus, June 2007

The Authentic Brand

Chapter 1:
Facing The Truth: There Are Too Many "Faceless" Companies

"There are too many faceless companies today. Businesses, regardless of size, must connect emotionally with their audiences, with people."
— John Rosica

Today's competitive business landscape demands differentiation. Companies must stand apart to be noticed. When evaluating the options—one can look at those brands or corporations that have done this exceptionally well and pinpoint the factors that have contributed to their success. In *The Authentic Brand* we go inside the minds of some of today's most prominent entrepreneurs to see how they achieved their success.

We begin by asking a simple question that many entrepreneurs ask: How can a company or brand stand apart when such a large number of competing companies and brands are vying for our attention?

One way of achieving this is to put a face on your company, and to give it an identity that separates it from the often faceless competition. As we have seen with the entrepreneurs featured in this book, sometimes that face is the entrepreneur's own!

As Jeff Taylor, founder of the Monster Board job-listing service

> **Today, among those faceless companies are too many who forego authenticity for homogeneity.**

and the first CEO of Monster.com, told us, "You've got to put yourself out in front of your brand."

Today, among those faceless companies are too many who forego authenticity for homogeneity. Just go online. Website after website touting a company's products or services looks just like the next. Strip malls are a great example of the vanilla retail landscape that has lined our roads from coast to coast. And beyond that, what percentage of the products, services or businesses are truly *authentic*? Is it two, or maybe three, percent?

Which insurance company should you select? Isn't that really based on price or your local insurance broker? What technology company should you hire? Isn't that hit or miss? What real-estate company will get your listing? Aren't most really the same? What brokerage firm should you trust? Do any stand apart for their integrity, compassion, exceptional service, or other attributes that immediately come to mind? What accounting firm stands out for these traits? We are sure that you get the idea that being truly *authentic* is uncommon.

In *The World Is Flat: A Brief History of the Twenty-First Century*, Thomas Friedman gives a couple of wonderful examples of people who are outstanding examples of authenticity in the form of spokespersons for their product. These people are so authentically engaging that they make you go out of your way to buy their product.

The first is a lemonade vendor who works the lower deck at Camden Yards during the Baltimore Oriole's home games. He has, as Friedman describes it, "perfected a dance routine around how he shakes and prepares the lemonade. He does a little jig and then high-fives you before he hands you the drink."

Friedman writes, "I love to watch him operate because all he is selling is water with sugar and a lemon in a plastic cup. It couldn't be more of a commodity. It couldn't be a more vanilla job. Yet I always notice that by the end of the game he is carrying around a wad of bills—and tips—that is thicker than any other vendor's I see."

Answering the question "Why?" Friedman explains that here is a man who has taken an ordinary job and has creatively put his personal touch on the way he delivers his product. Consumers, who could buy soft drinks or water from other vendors, patronize the lemonade man because, as Friedman points out, he puts a smile on your face.

Another example cited by Friedman is an African American woman who works at the Caribou Coffee outlet near his K Street office in Washington, D.C. As he describes her, "she goes out of her way to be helpful and asks me about myself—not in a phony, overtrained way, like the staff at the Ritz-Carlton, but in a sincere way that I find charming."

In both examples, Friedman might also have added the adjective *authentic.*

To solve the problem of facelessness, some companies have opted for using celebrity endorsers, such as professional athletes, to promote their products. Does this give you the idea that they are truly *authentic?*

In fact, studies—including those that led to creation of the National Credibility Index—have shown that celebrity product

> **By so closely identifying themselves with their products, these entrepreneurs add an emotional element and genuineness to their brand that is generally absent in the Brand Xs of the world.**

recommendations lack the level of credibility that is given to a product or company when the person responsible for the product puts his or her identity on the line to promote it. The Public Relations Society of America (PRSA) undertook the creation and development of the National Credibility Index to measure and track the extent to which the American public perceives its leaders and/or public figures to be believable sources of information and guidance on major issues. The study shows that business leaders, experts in a given field, and educators rank most credible, while celebrities and professional athletes rank towards the bottom of the list. At the top of the list are the people who are actually behind the company. What's more *authentic* than that?

The entrepreneurs with whom we spoke when writing this book have built successful brands while putting their own names and faces on the line. By so closely identifying themselves with their products, these entrepreneurs add an emotional element and genuineness to their brand that is generally absent in the Brand Xs of the world. Through this personal connection, these companies have turned out true consumer and customer advocates.

Many of the business leaders featured in this book demonstrate personalities that attract strong brand followings. One such example that demonstrates this is cookie magnate Wally "Famous" Amos. Working with my mentors and parents, Marilyn and John

Rosica, Wally made himself and his cookies into "stars." As John Rosica says, "Putting his 'face' in front of the brand"—through public appearances sampling cookies, spokesperson/media tours, events with Literacy Volunteers of America, reading to kids in schools and libraries nationwide, author tours (Wally has written several books), and greeting everyone with enthusiasm and charisma—was the key to his success. Amos's genuinely positive attitude and winning personality have been his trademarks, and he has remained in the public eye long after the sale of Famous Amos and the emergence of two other companies he has launched.

A spokesperson, remaining highly visible, adds a level of credibility and builds confidence among consumers or, in a business-to-business environment, customers. This principle applies online as well. Most e-commerce and corporate websites lack the personal touch. The remedy is simple—place your spokesperson prominently on your site with his or her story. This will help create a bond with your audience at a subconscious or biological level. According to Sinek and Dr. Andrea Simon, who are both anthropologists and experts in ethnography, the best and brightest companies have a knack for delivering an experiential advantage that creates a "stickiness factor" and fosters loyalty and positive word-of-mouth.

In the syllabus for an upper-level course in Customer Relationship Management at the McCombs School of Business at The University of Texas at Austin, Dr. Linda Golden, professor of business in the Department of Marketing, writes: "Customer Relationship Management involves building a bond with your customers by developing products and services directed toward satisfying marketplace wants and needs."

In her course description, Dr. Golden goes on to stress, "No matter what industry you are in, no matter what the nature of your firm is, and no matter what your legal organizational structure is, doing business in today's environment is increasingly complex, dynamic, and competitive. This necessitates that the firm, more than ever, be attuned to Customer Relationship Management."

The question is: How can a company or brand achieve this?

As we were speaking with the business leaders we have included in this book, we were curious to know how they felt about identifying their own personas with the identity of the companies they started. In our own public relations work, we have always felt that this is important, because having a prominent person associated with the company and its product or service is a great differentiator—and media relations strategy. We've found that when consumers—or whoever our clients' customers are—see this, they respond positively to the notion that someone is responsible for quality and that some real person is answerable.

Jerry Greenfield, the co-founder of Ben & Jerry's Homemade, told us: "I think that's true. There is a tradition among homemade ice cream parlors that they're named after the people who operate them. There was Steve's Ice Cream; there was Bob's Ice Cream, and whatever. When we were starting out as a homemade ice cream parlor, it was just a natural thing. It soon became clear that there are a lot of advantages to having it be named after real people, as opposed to fake people. There are a bunch of businesses that are named after fake people too, but having real people involved did let the customers know that you were standing behind the product, and that you believed in what you were doing."

"As they say in marketing," Ben Cohen, Jerry's partner, interjected, "it lends an air of *authenticity*."

When asked to comment on how the Ben & Jerry's name will help the legacy of the brand, now that neither Ben nor Jerry is directly involved with the brand, Jerry said that, "to a certain degree it depends on what the brand becomes."

Ben Cohen sees that the legacy of the Ben & Jerry's brand will be supported by retaining the goals and *ideals* that were important when Ben and Jerry themselves were still directly associated with the brand. These are, according to Ben, "finding new and innovative ways to solve social problems, and making better and better and more innovative flavors of ice cream."

By furthering new and innovative ways to resolve problems, and by continually improving their product, Ben and Jerry underscored their corporate image with a sense of genuineness.

Another example of the names of two founders who became the brand name is Kate Spade, the brand created by Kate Brosnahan and her then-future husband, Andy Spade. As Andy told us, "We took Kate's first name and my last name and combined them."

As he recalls, this apparently obvious choice was not, in fact, immediately obvious. "I liked Apple," he recalls. "I couldn't come up with another concept name like Apple. There were a couple of brands that we really liked. I have to say that we were inspired by Paul Smith as a company, and we were inspired by the French designer agnès b, who opened her first store in Soho in the 1980s. I've always liked those companies."

Both Andy and Kate agree that there is a level of authenticity associated with brands named for real people. "It lends credibility," Andy says. "It says that there is someone behind the brand."

In addition to Kate's name, Andy Spade cites Kate's design as being a big part of the success of the brand. Andy credits Kate herself with being the brand's best marketing tool. "A big part of it is obviously her," he explained. "She's definitely the best marketing tool we have. Public relations has been very good. The branding on the bag itself, just the Kate Spade label, was a huge, important part of our identity because every bag on the street was an ad for Kate Spade. People recognize our label just as they recognize features such as the Levi's red tab. We've heard that people have loved the advertising, and have been able to get a feeling for what the Kate Spade image is beyond a handbag. This helps really build the idea of Kate Spade being *beyond just a product-based company*, to more of a lifestyle company. The website has been tremendously helpful, and a great tool for us. Our retail stores are great. They are probably the best branding tools we have, beyond Kate herself."

Another woman whose name is identified with the company that she founded is Bobbi Brown. She started Bobbi Brown Essentials in 1991, and achieved such a degree of success that Estée Lauder acquired the firm in 1995. Even after the acquisition, the parent company retained Bobbi herself to manage it. The subsidiary is officially Bobbi Brown Cosmetics, but the brand is simply Bobbi Brown.

When we asked her how she came up with the idea of naming the company, she had a simple answer. "My mom and dad named it when I was born," she smiled.

In fact, she did not originally plan to use her own name.

"It was not my idea to call it 'Bobbi Brown' at all," she told us. In tracing the origins of her branding concept, she recalls that she was gradually convinced by others, including her husband and her creative staff, that it was a good idea to use her own name as the brand.

"I was already a working makeup artist who had my name in magazines," she explains. "I had a *Vogue* cover. I was pretty respected in the fashion industry, and the concept was of a makeup artist who does models. They told me, 'You need your name,' so I said, 'all right.'"

She recalls that the brand was originally called "Bobbi Brown Essentials." "At first, I was thinking of 'Basics,'" she told us, "because when the company started, we started with ten lipsticks. I was thinking of 'Basics,' which would have been a very different company. Then it became 'Essentials,' and then it was much more than that, so we dropped 'Essentials.'"

She explained to us that, in addition to word-of-mouth, public relations has been a vital branding tool for the company. Her own image as the image of the brand is a key to success. "I still do in-store appearances around the country about 20 times a year," she says. "Women are still coming up to me and saying, 'Oh, I brought you all the girls in my office;' 'My sister brought me in;' 'My daughter brought me in;' or 'Here's my Girl Scout troop.' It's so word-of-mouth."

Bobbi also considers giving away samples as an important part of word-of-mouth marketing. "I've also believed in giving a lot away," she told us. "From the beginning I sampled. I gave. I gave because I'm a giving person. I gave lipsticks to everybody and now when there are charity events, I give things... The company gives things. You cannot imagine how many new customers we've gotten because we always give away good stuff. A lot of companies give their slow movers away. We give our best stuff away."

From our experience in public relations, we have seen, first-hand, the power of sampling. It not only creates new customers and advocates, but it also drives media coverage and generates buzz.

When we asked Bobbi to reflect on how having a real name associated with a company lends credibility to a brand, she told us that she had never really quantified it, that for her it evolved organically through her career and the growth of her business.

"If I stand back and look at my business life, I've never calculated it," she says. "I became a beauty editor on *The Today Show* because I met the executive producer's grandmother in Florida. I met my first book agent on the beach. I'm working on a television show because I met someone. It's just weird the way things have happened. I've never calculated anything. I did lipsticks first because that was my first thought and everyone said 'It's so smart how you market it.' I didn't know what marketing was. I had never really heard the word. I didn't know what branding was. I did not have a marketing person for the first ten years in my business. I didn't know. Now I know, and now I can sit in meetings and talk with some intelligence about different things. How do you brand something? It has to be organic. I don't understand these people who think you can take something and brand it into something. It's got to be just organic. It's got to happen."

Indeed, the term "organic" is synonymous with genuine (or authentic)! As you can see, Brown was passionate about creating something bigger than just a company. She was fulfilling her true ambitions, and this brought the brand to life, generating loyal customers and revenues.

The notion of a brand's developing organically was certainly the case with Wally "Famous" Amos. The first African-American talent agent with the William Morris Agency, Amos had worked with numerous show-business personalities. He developed a reputation for being original and sending prospective clients a box of chocolate chip cookies—which he baked himself—as his calling card, along with his pitch for a meeting.

In 1975, he opened a store, and eventually he franchised his chocolate chip cookie retail concept. His friend, B.J. Gilmore, secretary to entertainer Quincy Jones, suggested that they go into business together selling cookies. As with many entrepreneurs who wound up naming their brand after themselves, Amos had not planned to do so at first.

As he recalls, "B.J. and I, were trying to figure out what to call this company, and she suggested, 'Why don't we call it 'Famous Amos Cookie Company'? It was still up in the air, so I went over to a friend of mine, Chuck Cassel, who was in the creative department at A&M Records. I said to him, 'Chuck, I've got a name man! It's 'Famous Amos Chocolate Chip Cookies'! Something was missing. Then Chuck grabbed a pen and paper and wrote 'The Famous Amos Chocolate Chip Cookie Company,' and that was it."

When asked whether he felt that putting his name on the product helps to lend credibility to the brand, he told us, "No question. For the last 30 years, I've had a good reputation and good integrity. People know me. When I started Famous Amos, my whole attitude

> **From our experience in public relations, we have seen, firsthand, the power of sampling. It not only creates new customers and advocates, but it also drives media coverage and generates buzz.**

> **He feels that the brand resonates with the consumer because of his personal connection with the brand.**

was to be in business to create friends, not to sell a product. For the last 30 years I've made a lot of friends, including people whom I've never met and will never meet. They consider themselves my friend and I consider them my friends also. I think there is real value in that."

He feels that the brand resonates with the consumer because of his personal connection with the brand. "They connect Wally Amos with it," he says, observing that many brands don't have that personal connection. "Toyota is a strong brand, but I don't think most people connect the founder, Kiichiro Toyoda, with the car. I don't think that people know that there was a 'Mr. Toyota' who started the company."

As he considered the legacy of the brand since it was acquired by Keebler (now part of Kellogg's) in 2001, Wally Amos was confident of its longevity. "It will go on," he says. "Famous Amos Cookies will be around. We did an exceptional job of establishing a really strong brand identity, and I believe that it will be around for years to come."

Amos's appetite for giving and making a mark, which led to his cookie calling cards, was heartfelt and genuine, and this provided entrepreneurial opportunity. Moreover, as you'll see in coming chapters, this altruism also led him to launch the legendary cause-marketing campaign that helped brand his company.

According to entrepreneur David Oreck, he had one very good reason for naming his company after himself when he formed the

Oreck Corporation in 1963. "Every other name was taken," he told us light-heartedly. "That's the truth. I thought of a lot of other names, but every time I went to check them, they were taken. I didn't like that idea at first, but I didn't have a choice. It was no brilliant thought. I was stuck. I needed a name."

We asked him whether any of the classic brands that were named for men such as Henry Ford or Walt Disney resonated with him. He replied that he really had not thought about the relationship of these names with their respective companies, but that, in retrospect, it helped him connect with these iconic brands.

Born in northern Minnesota, Oreck served in the U.S. Army Air Forces during World War II. When he was discharged from the service in 1946, he went to New York and was hired as a salesman with an RCA wholesaler. He worked his way up through the ranks until he became general sales manager. He was involved in the introduction of black-and-white television, color television, RCA microwave ovens, and various Whirlpool appliances.

"I was with RCA for 17 years before I started Oreck Corporation, which I did at the age of 40 in 1963," he explained, giving us a capsule overview of his long and successful career. "I've done this ever since. I'm not exactly a job jumper."

When Whirlpool was unable to do well with its upright vacuum cleaner, Oreck acquired the rights to the product and completely redesigned it. Initially, he marketed the Oreck machines only to the hotel industry, but they were such a hit that he soon began selling them to consumers as well. Oreck's firm became, and continues to be, a vertically integrated company, designing, manufacturing, and marketing its products.

"Our business is complicated," he explained. "I suppose most are, but we have a real vertical operation. We do everything: We manufacture, we design, we make our own tools, we have our own retail stores, and we create our own advertising and marketing. We even have our own school for educating our dealers, as well as our own people. It's called Oreck University."

Oreck's firm is one of only a few American companies still operating in such a fashion. He feels that, in order for him to ensure reliability and quality, it is important not to rely on overseas production outsourcing in the manufacture of his products and parts. He prefers to keep his operation under his own direct control.

Given some time to reflect on the choice of his own name for the company, David Oreck considers it a good decision. "I will say, in retrospect, that it was a good move," he explains. "I've always felt that, with the namelessness and facelessness of business, putting a name and a face to a product is a good idea. If you buy a new Buick and the darn thing doesn't work, whom do you call? General or Motors or whom? But if you buy an Oreck vacuum cleaner, you know where to call."

David Oreck does not take lightly the responsibility that goes along with an entrepreneur's having his name on a brand. "I think you have to set an example with your people," he cautioned. "Since they know that your name is on the check and your name is on the front door, you have to set more of an example than if it was just the Apex Company and you happen to be the CEO. It's just different. There are responsibilities that go along with it and, if you screw up it's your name that negatively impacts your company."

Unlike Bobbi Brown, David Oreck, or Ben and Jerry, Jeff Taylor deliberately chose not to use his own name or his own identity in naming his Monster Board job-search service, and later, Monster.

com. He explained that, like Larry Page and Sergay Brin when they named Google, he wanted a word that would stick in people's minds. "Monster has nothing to do with jobs," Taylor reflected. "Nobody really got it at the beginning. At first, people didn't like the name at all, but they remembered it. It's

> **"What I've found is that doing personal branding for the Monster brand was critical for keeping us out there."**
>
> **—Jeff Taylor**

probably the most powerful source of energy for the whole brand because it's memorable. People can embrace it and, as it's talked about, people will remember it. Calling the business 'Monster' was probably the single most important moment in the business."

For Taylor, a primary component of personal branding is public appearances. "In busier years, I'll probably speak about 70 times," he told us. "More than once a week, I'm in front of big groups. What I've found is that doing personal branding for the Monster brand was critical for keeping us out there."

Roxanne Quimby's story is a rags-to-riches example of using the image of a real person to grow what was literally a cottage industry into a major corporation. When she met Burt Shavitz in the early 1980s, he was an unassuming beekeeper living on a small farm near Garland, Maine. Roxanne was working three waitress jobs—and buying and selling at flea markets—to get by. Burt was selling his honey, but stockpiling his beeswax. She suggested that he start making candles, and soon they were making beeswax lip balm and the Burt's Bees line of natural personal-care products was born. By 1992, when Burt's Bees relocated to North Carolina, they had become a major success.

The combination of quality, caring, accountability and the human touch constitutes what we would classify as an _authentic_ brand.

In growing the company, Roxanne explains that originally she was selling quality, but by the 1990s, she realized that she had a good story, and began using public relations to brand the company. "Burt was a sage," she explains. "He said stuff that would hit you in the face. Public relations was the best marketing tool. We used personal appearances by Burt. We announced that Burt was coming, and consumers could meet him and get a T-shirt. We used third-party endorsements from beauty editors, plus grassroots sampling. We distributed millions of samples and educated retailers such as health-food stores about skin care. We used an emotional connection to the product, the human element, and caring about people's needs."

The combination of quality, caring, accountability, and the human touch constitutes what we would classify as _authentic_.

In developing the brand, she told us that Ben and Jerry had been her role models, just as Ben and Jerry told us that Wally Amos had been an important role model for them.

From Ben and Jerry, Roxanne told us that she "learned that you can do what you love and make money at it."

Jim Koch of the Boston Beer Company based his flagship brand on the well-known name of an early American patriot. Samuel Adams was an organizer of the Boston Tea Party, a signer of the Declaration of Independence, and a governor of Massachusetts who had also been active in the brewing industry around Boston in the eighteenth century. Koch's great-great grandfather had started a brewery in St. Louis in 1860, and Jim resurrected his recipe when he began brewing in Boston in 1985.

We asked him to reflect on which marketing tools had been the key to Boston Beer's branding and marketing success.

"We started with the product," he explained. "Aside from the product, it has been basic street selling—retail execution. It has been a matter of getting our product into the right bars, and getting the tap handles visible at eye level. There are lots of little breweries. Sam Adams has been one that stood out. It had a lot to do with the beer.

"I did radio commercials myself in the beginning," Jim Koch told us when we asked him to comment on other tools that he had used to connect himself personally with his customers and build a loyal brand following. "I got on the radio and talked about the beer. It was so different than the normal beer advertisement. My personal involvement was real. I wasn't some Bartles and Jaymes type of character. I was actually the guy who started making the beer in his kitchen, and who still makes it. I would talk about the things I worried about, like the culture and the quality of the beer. It seemed to work because it was genuine. It wasn't something that came from an ad agency."

Bartles and Jaymes, to which Jim Koch referred, is a line of flavored wine coolers and malt-beverage products from the E. and J. Gallo Winery, California. In contrast to the authentic pitchman approach exemplified by people such as Dave Thomas of Wendy's Hamburgers or Jim Koch, the Bartles and Jaymes brand manufactured a pair of spokesmen who were deliberately designed to appear authentic, but who were not. From 1985 through 1991, Gallo aired a series of television spots which featured a pair of folksy older gen-

> **Baldwin uses the word "quality," which, as we've stated, is a characteristic that speaks to your customers' intelligence and fosters an authentic experience. He credits the connectivity of both brands with unparalleled product quality *and* excellent customer service.**

tlemen who were discussing their product. As they sat on the front porch of what appeared to be a farmhouse, Frank Bartles and Ed Jaymes came across not only as unimpeachably authentic, but also downright charming. The only problem was that they were actually actors David Joseph Rufkahr and Dick Maugg. Created for Gallo by Hal Riney and Partners of San Francisco, the ads won an Andy Award in 1986 for best print and broadcast advertising campaign.

However, as clever as the campaign had been, Frank Bartles and Ed Jaymes created a backlash within the advertising community. Their lasting legacy has been to underscore the value of using compelling stories that are *truly* authentic to promote products. Though exceedingly clever, the Bartles and Jaymes ads created a fad, not a trend in advertising. They did not create a lasting or genuine brand that spoke to their customers' intelligence.

Jerry Baldwin, one of the original founders of Starbucks, and later principal of Peet's Coffee and Tea, tells the story of how he and his colleagues chose the Starbucks corporate name as they prepared to open their first location in 1971.

"We concluded that it should be somebody's surname," he recalls. "Our names together—Baldwin, Bowker, and Siegel—sounded like a law firm, and none of the names individually was particularly good, so we picked a great name with Starbucks."

Though Starbucks had a name, the partners did not immediately exploit its public relations potential. "In the beginning, we hid behind the product, and didn't concentrate on communication and image," Jerry Baldwin recalls. "Gordon Bowker had been a writer since high school and college. He was the writing half of a corporate communications firm and was a journalist as well. His partner in the communications firm designed the original Starbucks logo."

Eventually, however, they began to capitalize on the image that they were creating. "We had a good logo and we had a good name," Baldwin says. "We had the quality and we tried to create the decor in the store that supported what we were doing. We tried to make the image appear timeless, and not fixed in time. A design professional can look at a corporate logo or a typeface and say that it's from a particular time. When we bought Peet's, it had one of those 1973 logos, and we changed it. There are a lot of color and typography decisions in store design. When I was making the decisions, we always used serif type faces because sans serif type is cold and modern. You want to look awake without looking too industrial or too cool. You want to be warm and timeless."

Baldwin uses the word "quality," which, as we've stated, is a characteristic that speaks to your customers' intelligence and fosters an authentic experience. He credits the connectivity of both brands with unparalleled product quality *and* excellent customer service.

Like Google and Monster, Starbucks is a brand name that did not *initially* relate to the product, but it was a memorable word that eventually came to be synonymous with the product. Today, each of these brands offers both quality and a unique customer experience.

Peet's, meanwhile, is named for Alfred Peet, who founded the company in 1966. After nearly two decades and an interim owner, Jerry Baldwin purchased the company in 1984.

"In the case of Peet's, what probably makes the name strong is that he was an actual person," Jerry explained. "Although it's always misspelled, it is not often mispronounced and it's short. Those are positive things."

On the point of naming a company after an actual person, Baldwin sees both sides. "I can think of many examples of successful companies that are not named for people, so I would say that it's not that crucial," he reflects. "A few generations later, who remembers? Think about the American car brands. How many are named after people and how many of them aren't? There were a pile of them that were named after people, and that doesn't mean anything anymore. Who was Walter Dodge anyway? However, it is crucial to stand out in front of the brand and be accountable."

David Neeleman, the founder and CEO of JetBlue Airways, has never been shy about being the spokesman for his company. Nor is he shy about saying that it is he who is accountable and ultimately responsible for serving JetBlue customers. When he spoke with us, he began with the story of his early days of developing his brand. He had gone to New York to begin discussing branding concepts and corporate names with major advertising agencies.

"It was a very interesting experience, coming off the turnip truck from Utah and going to New York," he modestly recalls in the course of discussing the many things that he did before he started JetBlue. "The agencies said, 'Hey we're going to make you …We're going to make your brand… We're the essence of who you're going to become." That just totally offended me. I thought, what the heck are you talking about? You're not going to be serving my customers, you're not going to be booking my customers, and you're not going to be flying them."

Neeleman went on to explain that he saw an advertising agency as the "wrapper." He told them that it would be he and his team who would be delivering on the brand. "You can help us create a good logo, a good slogan, a good ad campaign, good uniforms, and all that kind of stuff," Neeleman said. "But we're running the brand, not you."

He believed when he started the company, and he believes today, that a brand name is less important than the integrity behind the name. The integrity, he feels, speaks to his customers' intelligence. As he puts it, "Ultimately it's how you treat your customers. We could have named the airline anything we wanted to name it, but people will look up to it because of the way we serve every single customer. Look at a name like 'Google.' It could be called just about anything and it would be successful because of what it *does*."

Having named his company, Neeleman believes that supporting that brand name is vitally important to the image of the airline. He is very focused on public relations, and he relies heavily on media relations. This, he feels, has contributed greatly to his success.

"I have brand people here now who are every bit as focused on the brand as the people at Disney or at Virgin," he explains. "They're very focused on how the JetBlue brand is displayed, but ultimately it's how you treat your customers."

While Neeleman has been challenged by adversity, his genuine commitment to his customers and to creating a positive and unique experience for people who fly JetBlue is unwavering.

The Authentic Brand

Chapter 2:
Doing Good to Do Well:
How Cause-Related Marketing Builds
Brands and Good Will

As discussed in my book, *The Cause Marketing Handbook: How Doing Good Means Doing Well*, cause marketing is one of the most important and powerful marketing tools in existence. Whether you call it corporate social responsibility or corporate philanthropy, it is a process that links for-profit businesses with not-for-profit organizations for mutual benefit.

Embracing a cause makes good business sense. Few things build brand devotion among today's increasingly hard-to-please consumers like a company's proven commitment to a worthy charity. In fact, most people prefer to do business with a company that stands for something beyond profits. According to recent studies, nearly three quarters of the United States population, particularly women, prefer to do business with socially responsible companies.

In our many decades of experience in public relations and brand-building, we have seen time and again that cause-related marketing builds customer loyalty and good will. It also improves employee morale and dedication, inspires others to get philanthropically and communally involved, and it attracts considerable media coverage. The media love human interest stories and cause-marketing campaigns are designed with an emotional element built in.

Embracing a cause makes good business sense. Few things build brand devotion among today's increasingly hard-to-please consumers like a company's proven commitment to a worthy charity.

Today, corporations and nonprofits are forming mutually beneficial strategic alliances. The non-profit organization benefits from increases in awareness, in donations, and in volunteerism. Meanwhile, corporations infuse a philanthropic agenda into their marketing strategy, which results in more than just advantageous media attention. Without sending an overt commercial message, the company is able to avoid or manage crises, increase sales and customer loyalty, improve employee morale and retention, and heighten brand awareness. *The Cause Marketing Handbook* provides a step-by-step process for implementing such a campaign. (For more information, please visit causemarketingbook.com.)

Only 10 to 15 percent of charitable giving comes from corporations. Individuals remain the biggest givers. However, the cause-marketing trend is becoming so much a part of today's corporate culture that companies are not just encouraged but also are *expected,* to "give back." Without their having embraced a philosophy of corporate social responsibility, they are held under public scrutiny. Alternatively, companies reap public relations rewards when they are seen as championing environmental, cure-finding, or human-rights causes.

As we point out in *The Cause Marketing Handbook,* Henry Ford once observed that the one rule for the industrialist was to

"Make the highest quality goods possible at the lowest cost possible, paying the highest wages possible." Certainly it is hard to argue with quality, pricing, and providing your workers with a suitable paycheck—but today, that's not enough. Today's business-as-usual industrialists are often *perceived* as greedy and insensitive. Conversely, studies prove that today people are unlikely to react negatively, and are more willing to pay more for a product or service, if they believe that the person or the company behind the brand is generous and charitable. With a solid public-relations and cause-marketing program, price is less of an issue. Brands such as Newman's Own, as well as Ben & Jerry's, are good examples of this.

Microsoft founder Bill Gates exemplifies an industrialist who was once thought of as greedy. He had become the world's richest man while building Microsoft into the leading software company internationally, but, in the 1990s, the entrepreneur who was once praised as a rags-to-riches success story was now viewed as a villain. Gates found himself the target of accusations that his company was ruthless in achieving global dominance. Microsoft was accused of such outrages as "unfair competition," "predator pricing," and wielding "monopolistic power." The software giant was vilified for going only as far as Henry Ford would have gone—creating a popular product at an accessible price. As Bill Gates found, success breeds contempt. Realizing that businesses will do well by doing good, the entrepreneur counterattacked by reinventing his public image as that of a philanthropist, a brilliant business-saving strategy.

In 2000, the Microsoft founder and his wife created the Bill and Melinda Gates Foundation "to help reduce inequities in the United States and around the world." Today, it is the largest charitable foun-

> **Realizing that businesses will do well by doing good, the entrepreneur Bill Gates counterattacked by reinventing his public image as that of a philanthropist, a brilliant business-saving strategy.**

dation in the world, and Bill Gates is no longer seen as a greedy corporate giant, but rather recognized as one of the nation's top philanthropists. It is no coincidence that Microsoft's quarterly earnings continue to rise. Just as Gates came to realize that he could do well by, again, doing good, entrepreneurs can take the lesson that they can do well by emulating the world's most successful entrepreneur.

As Gates would tell you, cause marketing is more than simply donating a percentage of your company's profit to charity. It has a profit motive that even the freest of free-market libertarians can embrace. Cause marketing positions a social agenda as a platform for a marketing campaign. Corporate social responsibility may focus on doing good for the sake of doing good, but cause marketing uses doing good as a means toward doing well.

Jerry Greenfield, the co-founder of Ben & Jerry's, cited Henry Ford's maxim, but agreed that going the extra step is essential. "Our mission statement is a little different from most," he told us. "Most business mission statements talk about creating great products and satisfying your customers' needs and exceeding expectations. Delighting your customers is a wonderful thing to do. This is the first in our three-part mission statement. The product mission is incredibly high-quality ice cream; an economic mission is a fair return for our investors or stakeholders, but there is also a social mission for the company. This is the part that was different from most other businesses. We were very explicit that the social mission was very important to the other parts of the mission. They were all interrelated."

John Mackey, the owner and founder of Whole Foods, has written that, "There can be little doubt that a certain amount of corporate philanthropy is simply good business and works for the long-term benefit of the investors."

Mackey demonstrated this when he created "Five Percent Days" to introduce new shoppers to his grocery stores. On these days, each Whole Foods store donates five percent of its total sales to specified nonprofit organizations. Whole Foods selects the nonprofits in part by their number of donors, who are contacted and encouraged to shop at Whole Foods on the "Five Percent Days," thereby supporting their cause and increasing profits for Whole Foods. As its loyal customers well know, Whole Foods, along with many of the companies founded by the entrepreneurs whom we interviewed for this book, charge a premium for high-quality, authentic products. This clearly demonstrates that price doesn't have to be a factor if quality, good service, and authenticity prevail.

Modern marketing is much more than billboards, print, broadcast, and direct mail. Consumers are increasingly ignoring the messages that come at them from the traditional directions. According to psychologist Mihaly Csikszentmihalyi, we are able to process only about 100 of the two million bits of information available each second through the five senses. Consumers have learned the art of selective filtering to tune out traditional advertising. With the sudden rise in popularity of TiVo and DVRs, people aren't even seeing that long-time advertising standby, the television commercial.

> **Consumers have learned the art of selective filtering to tune out traditional advertising.**

Even in the cases where consumers do see and notice traditional advertising, they often react negatively to the onslaught of unwanted junk mail, email, and pushy telemarketers. In short, not only is it getting harder for companies to reach consumers, but also they are finding consumers increasingly unreceptive, even when the message does get through.

Companies are realizing that, for a marketing campaign to succeed, the company must clearly demonstrate what is in it for the end-user and de-commercialize the commercial message. It must take the sales out of the sales pitch.

Cause marketing does just this. It convinces a consumer to buy a product or use a service without directly pitching the product or service. By leveraging the public's desire for companies to engage in socially responsible behavior, companies that use cause marketing find that it is a form of subliminal messaging. Consumers would much rather buy the products of a company that they perceive as unselfish. Since Bill Gates started his foundation, Microsoft is now considered a good corporate citizen.

Not all philanthropists set up foundations as their means of doing good; some create commercial companies and channel profits of the company into doing good. An excellent example is Academy Award-winning actor Paul Newman, who founded the Newman's Own brand of food products in 1982. The brand started with salad dressing, and later expanded to include pasta sauce, as well as cat food, coffee, cookies, fruit juices, iced tea, lemonade, limeade, popcorn, salsa, and other products. The company is a for-profit corporation, with Paul Newman receiving all the proceeds. He then donates 100 percent of those proceeds, after taxes, to educational and charitable purposes. According to the Newman's Own website, the franchise resulted in more than $200 million in its first two dozen years. Some of the charitable giving goes to the PEN/Newman's Own Award, presented each year to a U.S. resident who has defended the First Amendment right to freedom of expression as it applies to the written word. Newman's Own also sponsors the Hole-in-the-Wall Gang Camp in Connecticut, a summer camp for seriously ill children that Newman co-founded in 1986.

As stated on the company's website, "Newman's Own was supposed to be a tiny boutique operation—parchment labels on elegant wine bottles of antique glass. We expected train wrecks along the way and got, instead, one astonishment followed by another. We flourished like weeds in the garden of Wishbone, like silver in the vaults of finance. A lot of the time we thought we were in first gear we were really in reverse, but it didn't seem to make any difference."

In a textbook public relations program that is still used as a case study in university marketing classrooms today, my firm worked with Famous Amos Cookies to develop grassroots media events, a spokesperson tour, and a strategic cause-marketing tie-in with Literacy Volunteers of America to

Companies are realizing that for a marketing campaign to succeed, the company must clearly demonstrate what is in it for the end-user and de-commercialize the commercial message. It must take the sales out of the sales pitch.

tell the brand's story and maintain visibility. *Snack Food Magazine* called this effort "a truly classic public relations campaign… one of the most successful campaigns in the history of the food business." When the brand was purchased in 1998 by Keebler, The Famous Amos brand, which began and operated for decades without an advertising budget, was valued at approximately $200 million.

By selecting a charity about which you are passionate, cause-related marketing can be emotionally and economically rewarding. It is a way to build a business that parallels your personal and corporate values and beliefs. If your cause also resonates with your target audience, your activities will create tremendous good will and media attention.

Whether championing an environmental cause, mentoring those in need of hope, supporting literacy, or being community-involved, these successful entrepreneurs have closely identified themselves with charities about which they feel strongly. This commonality has helped our interviewees connect with loyal customers and create a cachet surrounding the products and services each represents. Perhaps most important, these efforts have gone a very long way toward creating good will.

Our look at cause-related marketing provides an insight into the interpersonal skills and beliefs of these successful business leaders, who are clearly aware that consumers prefer to do business with companies closely associated with a cause. In fact, studies have shown that more than three quarters of those surveyed would even pay more for a product because of that association. For example, the recent Cone Corporate Citizenship Study reveals that eight in ten Americans say that corporate support of causes wins their trust in that company, a 21-percent increase since 1997.

This study and its research, which spans over a decade, show that, in today's climate, more than ever before, companies must get involved with social issues in order to protect and enhance their reputations. As our society continues to become busier and busier, people have limited hours and resources to give. Therefore, in many cases, customer loyalty among cause-involved businesses improves as a convenient way for a customer to give—and feel good about giving—without sacrificing personal time or energy.

While many companies and their founders and CEOs are involved on some level with philanthropy, many do not utilize cause marketing strategically at the corporate level to inspire their workforce, customers, and the masses to give back or get involved.

As we've noted, the Cone Corporate Citizenship Study demonstrates that consumers consciously align themselves with cause-oriented businesses. Indeed, the study also found that the proportion of consumers who said they were likely to switch away from a brand that is not associated with a cause—assuming that it was of the same price and quality—increased from 65 percent in 1999 to 86 percent just five years later. Astute business owners know and understand this phenomenon and plan accordingly.

All of the entrepreneurs whom we interviewed for this book have closely identified themselves in one way or another with charities about which they feel strongly. They all explained that this has helped them to connect with loyal customers, as well as to create a cachet surrounding the products and services that they represent.

Because of our passion for helping nonprofits, a portion of the royalties from the sales of this book will be donated to charities named by each of our entrepreneur interviewees.

For instance, as Bobbi Brown explained to us, "I'm a big believer in giving back. I finish every speech with my secret of the universe, which is the more you give, the more you get. It's true."

When it comes to charitable involvement, she is very deliberate about keeping her business and personal activities separate. "Personally, my husband and I are very philanthropic," she told us. "We do a lot of things for our community. My husband is on three or four boards. I'm always the class mom, and any time there's a note that comes home saying that they need coats, or they need this or that, I'm on the phone. I look at myself as Robin Hood sometimes. My friends have so much, so I'm constantly collecting."

Bobbi Brown explains that she personally likes helping people. "From my tailor who wants her daughter to have a job, to someone who has a friend who had cancer who needs makeup—I do those kinds of things pretty effortlessly," she says.

On the corporate side, she explains that her company makes sizable donations of cosmetics. "We've adopted programs, and we have makeup lines affiliated with them," she told us. "The biggest one is Dress For Success, an organization that helps women in need get back on their feet. Everyone who goes through the program—and there are a lot—gets a Bobbi Brown makeover and a bag of makeup so she can do her own. A couple of times a year, I do events where I bring my makeup artists in. You get your makeup done and all the money goes to Dress for Success. You're encouraged to clean out your closet. So they literally walk away with van-loads of stuff for the women."

Another of Bobbi's corporate programs is a partnership with the Jane Addams High School, a vocational school in the South Bronx. "I'll do anything from giving master classes to donating Estée Lauder products," she says enthusiastically. "I encourage my employees to bring stuff to donate to their nurseries, like diapers and bottles and clothes. We do that a couple times a year, plus we have the students come in to our headquarters regularly, and we send different departments from Bobbi Brown Cosmetics into the school."

The third program that Bobbi Brown supports on a corporate level is the Fresh Air Fund, a charity dating back more than a hundred years that was created to help inner-city children enjoy experiences outside urban environments. "We created a special lip gloss and gave all the proceeds to the Fresh Air Fund," she says enthusiastically. "I also mentor a bunch of young girls who are starting their businesses. One of them, who makes soaps, makes our sandbar soap."

Bobbi Brown is also keen on personally maintaining a good working environment within her own organization. "I'm just a natural-born mother-nurturer," she told us. "I constantly give back to the people around me unless I'm completely overwhelmed and it's December and I can't deal. We try to do things special in the office, whether it's ordering lunch for everybody because each one is overworked or buying the public relations department massages at the end of Fashion Week. We constantly do things like that, but to me this isn't so much a matter of 'giving back,' as it's just being the right kind of person."

We agree with Bobbi. From our experience, corporate philanthropy should be strategic and purposeful, although we recommend that it is best for business owners to partner with a primary cause in order to "own" that association in the minds of their customers.

For Wally "Famous" Amos, the primary cause has always been literacy. "I was a high school dropout," he explains. "I didn't have a

From our experience, corporate philanthropy should be strategic and purposeful, although we recommend that it is best for business owners to partner with a primary cause in order to "own" that association in the minds of their customers.

lot of formal education, but I knew that education in the academic sense was important. Knowledge is important and you need to have access to it, so you can use it. The literal translation of 'educate' is to 'extract.' It doesn't mean to memorize a lot of books, and that's what a lot of education is today."

At the recommendation of Rosica Strategic Public Relations, Wally held a series of events at public sites, such as libraries and state houses, in cities across America. The media events dramatically featured Wally with a pair of bolt cutters, "cutting the bonds of illiteracy." Subsequently he became the national spokesperson for Literacy Volunteers of America, along with Barbara Bush, who learned about Literacy Volunteers through our cause-marketing agency.

"You have to advocate the cause and support it through your actions," he says emphatically. "When I started Famous Amos, we started promoting literacy. We had a small section in our store where anyone could read to kids. I got involved in promoting literacy because I think a business should be used for the greater good, and to give back to the community." As you will see in coming sections of this book, many of our entrepreneurs focus on more than building just sales or profits.

Jim Koch is active in Share Our Strength, a national nonprofit that inspires and organizes individuals and businesses to share their strengths in innovative ways to help eliminate hunger in America. Its programs are Taste of the Nation, the foremost culinary benefit supporting the fight to end hunger; the Great American Bake Sale, a grassroots campaign to end childhood hunger; and Operation Frontline, a nutrition-education program.

"We've just been very lucky that we're in a position where we can do some meaningful things," Koch says modestly. "As a publicly traded company, we do have to be careful about whose money we are giving away. I also have private charities and initiatives that I support with my own money. I can be a philanthropic hero, but I would be giving away other people's money if I did it solely through the business. Within the company, we try to work with charities that fit our business. We've been very involved over the years with cause marketing. That's been our mainstay for 25 years. We're very passionate about it ourselves; it charges us up."

Meanwhile, Koch's wife, Cynthia Fisher, is the entrepreneur who founded ViaCell, a publicly traded biotechnology company focused on enabling the widespread use of human cells as medicine. ViaCell provides umbilical-cord blood stem-cell banking through its Viacord Service and is developing a pipeline of proprietary stem-cell-product candidates intended to address cancer, cardiac disease, and diabetes. With her company, there is a built-in cause—saving lives.

Ben Cohen and Jerry Greenfield, who were inspired in part by the cause-marketing program we created for Wally Amos, are not only recognized for their innovative brands of ice cream, but also perhaps even better known for their giving back. Central to the mission of Ben & Jerry's has been a deep respect for individuals inside and outside the company, and a support for the communi-

Like many successful entrepreneurs, Hirshberg brings public relations into play to promote his community involvement and what is important to him.

ties of which they are a part. From the beginning, the company has focused on children and families, the environment, and sustainable agriculture on family farms.

"One primary inspiration for our cause involvement was Wally Amos' commitment to literacy," Jerry told us.

Gary Hirshberg, whose Stonyfield Farm yogurt empire essentially began as a family farm, explains that he puts his causes where his brand is. "We use our packaging," he told us. "We use our lids unabashedly to talk about the causes that we care about. There is a trite saying that 'Your package is your most critical point of contact,' and I take that pretty seriously. Your consumer will see your package far more than they'll ever see your advertising or anything else. I think that's key. The field marketing and the sampling are monstrous. It's a really big thing for us."

As you can see, here is another example of how sampling creates loyalty and brand awareness.

Imitation is the most sincere form of flattery, and Hirshberg went on to tell us how the concept of using yogurt packaging to promote cause awareness spread within the industry. "Yoplait dedicated their lids to breast cancer several years ago, and there is no question of where they got that idea," he remarked. "A number of former Yoplait execs told me they took one look at Stonyfield and our rate of growth, and they said 'Let's do this. What can we own?' I don't want to take anything away from them. It's fabulous they put millions into breast cancer, although there was an obvious connection to be made. They sell primarily to women, and this is a known threat to women. More power to them, though. I give them all the credit. Dannon is now doing the same thing on its packaging, talking about lighter weight packaging, and removing the over-cap. That backs up what is essentially a cost-cutting move on their part. But it's something that we did years ago!"

Reflecting on this "sincere flattery," he says, "Trust me, I love that these companies are copying us. My mission is not just to grow the biggest or fastest-growing yogurt brand. It's to change the way we *all* do business. That's where we get our real leverage in affecting change. We have to undo a generation of destructive post-industrial-revolution commerce here."

Like many successful entrepreneurs, Hirshberg brings public relations into play to promote his community involvement and what is important to him. He tells a story about one day when he picked up his seventh-grade son after school.

"I asked him what he had for lunch that day," Gary told us. "He said that he had pizza, chocolate milk, and Skittles. Here I am putting out organic, healthy food and my own kid is eating this. So I called the school nutritionist and asked whether there was something we could do about it."

"Gary, you know I love your yogurt," the nutritionist replied, as many people had. "I personally eat it every day, but if it's healthy it won't sell in schools. The kids won't buy it."

"That's the kind of biased world we're in," Hirshberg said, shaking his head. "Every single parent thinks about this. It's like a blind spot that we all face every single day when we send our kids off to school. We all know our schools are under-funded, so I launched a healthy vending program. We put 40 machines with all-natural products out there in schools across the country. Those 40 machines have won us—I'm now speaking the language of public relations here—53 million media impressions. When we launch our healthy vending program in a new school system, we are not surprised anymore to find news crews from five television stations. In other words, every major network and some cable stations are there with their cameras in our faces, hanging on our every word."

As much as he finds media attention desirable and beneficial to his brand, Hirshberg often opens his press conference at these events by saying "Listen guys, I love that you're here, but to be honest I can't wait until the day when having healthy food is not news." When he says this, he is being absolutely sincere.

He reflects that this program, and what it has done for his brand, began with his being a concerned father, not a business person. "I'm just lucky enough to have some business clout and the ability to do something about it. Why has it earned us immense amounts of press? It's not only topical, it's genuine. It's a real solution."

Jeff Taylor of Monster.com has personally dedicated many hours of volunteer time to helping kids get a good start with business experiences. He is a member of the Suskenini Arts Board, and he is on the national board of Junior Achievement. Taylor is also active with Boston-based Year Up, a one-year, intensive training program that provides young urban adults with a unique combination of technical and professional skills, college credits, and a paid corporate apprenticeship. When asked to which charity he would like some of the proceeds of this book to go, he named the "Team Adventure" organization, which operates the 110-foot racing catamaran aptly named Team Adventure. As he explained it, "Team

Adventure actually helps kids. They take kids out on the water and give them a great experience."

David Neeleman of JetBlue Airways reflects that, when he was in his mid-thirties, he discovered that the personal need to make money was no longer as important in his life as it once had been. "I had $25 million in Southwest Airlines stock and that was all the money I ever needed to live on and to raise my family," he explains. "So, it's not really something that governs my life. I'm continually disturbed by CEOs who continue to get large bonuses, large stock options, and big salaries. Their people don't respect them anymore. It's really something that concerns me greatly, and I don't want to be that kind of person. I tell our pilots that I had all the money I ever needed before I came to work here. I'm not here to get myself rich; I'm here to build a great company that you work for. I've got a lot of money in JetBlue stock, but I'm going to give it all away."

In the meantime, he tries to balance his philanthropy with the age-old problem of teaching his nine children the value of money. "There are a lot of conflicting things that I think about all the time," he says. "But I'm doing the best I can to teach my kids right and to respect the stewardship of money and also at the same time share with others those things that I've learned and try and make their lives better."

Neeleman is justifiably proud of his company's own JetBlue Crewmember Crisis Fund (JCCF), which provides money to JetBlue employees—known as "crewmembers"—in time of catastrophic need. His own personal generosity to the fund is well known. "You just get along better with pilots if they know that the CEO gives away his own salary to the JCCF. You ask them to put in five bucks a paycheck knowing that their five bucks will really become ten bucks because the president is matching it with his salary."

The fund has raised in excess of $800,000 annually in recent years, and the average grant to a crewmember is about $33,000. As Neeleman says, "I want our people coming here knowing that, if they do a good job, if they have a great attitude, if they show up to work on time with a good attitude, they're always going to have a job. They're going to have health insurance, and if they have a catastrophic event that's not covered by insurance, there is a foundation, an organization that will step in and help them."

Neeleman is also involved in a variety of other causes and charities. He donates money and time to spread the word about Attention Deficit Disorder, and he donates to the Perpetual Education Fund, a program of The Church of Jesus Christ of Latter-Day Saints—better known as the Mormon Church—of which Neeleman is a member. The fund provides loans to vocational school and university students in Bolivia, Brazil, Chile, Mexico, Peru, and the Philippines. Neeleman has earmarked his donations to Brazil, where he was born and where he once served as a Mormon missionary.

"I've donated millions to the fund," Neeleman told us. "There are about 600 kids who are in college because of it. These kids are coming up from the ghettos, and they are able to get a better standard of living. Every time we deliver a Brazilian-made Embraer airplane, we're going to give $10,000 to a scholarship for people in a different program in Brazil. We really do value our community, and give back to our community."

Starbucks co-founder Jerry Baldwin had a different take when we asked him to give us his thoughts on "giving back."

"I've always hated that expression," he said succinctly. "I don't think I have anything to give back because I didn't take anything."

He hastens to add that the involvement of his businesses in their communities has been "one of mutual respect and mutual benefit all along. To me it's enlightened self-interest to try to invest in the communities where we do business, whether it's buying or selling. If you really think your objective is purely charitable giving, then your donation should be anonymous. That's what I think."

Personally, Baldwin is a director of TechnoServe, a non-governmental, nonprofit organization whose mission is to build businesses that create jobs, income, opportunity, and economic growth in developing countries. TechnoServe notes that, despite the best efforts of the international donor community and development agencies over the past four decades, the average person in the developing world today is, at best, only moderately better off than he or she was in 1960. The objective of TechnoServe is, therefore, to provide the hardworking men and women in developing countries with the tools and the means to participate in and benefit from the global economy. TechnoServe's strategy for generating economic growth in developing countries is based on a market-driven, business-oriented approach. This approach involves providing local entrepreneurs with business-plan development, financial and commercial linkages, market research, market linkages, operational consulting, and supply-chain management.

In a hands-on role, Baldwin and Stephen Gluck, the former president of Cargill's Coffee Department, have traveled to places such as El Salvador, Nicaragua, Peru, and Tanzania to directly advise TechnoServe staff and clients on-site.

Andy Spade voiced a similar reaction to the concept of "giving back." As he put it, "We give back strategically. We support causes that relate to our business. And then, personally, we support causes we believe in, like the New York Center for Children, the ASPCA, and others."

Having said that, he went on to explain that the decisions that he and Kate Spade made to support causes have generally related to the arts and design.

"We're big supporters of the Museum of Modern Art, and of the Whitney Museum of American Art in New York," he said. "Our partner is on the board of the Parsons School of Design here in New York. We're very engaged with an organization called Public Color that brings color and life to schools. This relates to our business, which has a lot to do with color and fabric. We're also very involved in many other causes that generally tend to be skewed toward the arts, creativity, and design. This is very, very important to us."

Spade went on to stress the importance that he and Kate place on their vision of their company and its mission statement.

"We've placed a lot of importance on it since the day we started," he explained. "One of the things we do is manifest that idea. We always wanted to have a positive, successful business. We always first thought of ourselves as creative people. I never wanted to go out being known as a savvy businessman; that was never my goal in life. My goal was to be a really smart, innovative, fair person who wants to have a business that is successful. We would not compromise the culture of the company for the success of the company, and that may seem like a bad business decision, but ultimately it pays off."

He added that the company gives out an etiquette book when new employees join Kate Spade. "We've actually written books on manners and published them within the company," he told us. "We have an orientation video which speaks to the idea of being smart and respectful in business. It isn't soft; it's actually a great business tool in that it helps to recruit people. People want to work for intelligent, respectful people."

As with Kate Spade and JetBlue, Roxanne Quimby at Burt's Bees gives back by having created two foundations, one for families and another that focuses on environmental causes. Among the latter, Quimby highlights the effort to save open spaces. In fact, her foundation has purchased 50,000 acres and is restoring a wildlife habitat.

Burt's Bees was also recently a sponsor of the San Francisco Green Festival and Green Business Conference, and is a supporter of Co-op America's Green Business efforts. In practicing what it preaches, the company proudly boasts that "We don't just talk about saving the environment; we actually help protect it! For starters, we are passionate in our efforts to stay on the forefront of sustainable, recyclable, and reusable packaging technologies. Around the office, we recycle our toner cartridges, print on both sides of our printer paper, turn lights off when leaving the room, and always make sure that our trash cans are much less full than the recycle bin! It's the small things that make a difference; every bee knows that."

David Oreck believes that giving back is important, and his philosophy on the subject is summarized by the old proverb that says "Give a man a fish and you feed him for a day... Teach a man to fish and you feed him for a lifetime."

As he told us, "I think that I can be of most use in helping young people and people in business by telling them what I did and how I did it. I tell them what worked for me, and I tell them that if I did it, then they can surely do it too."

Oreck went on to underscore his belief that the United States is still the land of opportunity, an entrepreneur-friendly environment. "I feel very keenly that only in America can these things happen," he stressed. "There are millions of people all over the world waiting to come to America, but there are no lines of people waiting to leave, despite our shortcomings."

Putting his money where his ideals are, he reinforced the commitment that Oreck has made to manufacture its vacuum cleaners in the United States. "We're one of the few, and I'm proud of that fact," he told us. "I feel very strongly that we need to be more supportive of America, of our countrymen."

David Oreck's mission statement is simple. "I think that running a successful business is a mission in itself," he says succinctly. "Certainly against formidable competition it is. The credo that has worked for us, and which permeates the company, is to serve the customer well, and the customer is right. *Period.*"

As Nordstrom continuously demonstrates, for him, giving back also means giving quality to the customer. "Serving the customer begins with making a good product and, because it's a good product, to guarantee it longer than anybody else and to service it longer than others do. I don't care when they bought it, if they've got a point, we lean toward them and we fix it, replace it, or we give them their money back."

He went on to reflect on how his ideals about customer service have permeated the company. "I like to feel that has trickled down to our people all along the lines," he tells us. "Our customer service is very good. We bend over backwards to make it right. Serving the customer begins when a customer walks into one of our factory showrooms, of which we have several hundred all over the country," he explained. "If some-one were to buy something, we'll carry it to his or her car. If someone comes into the parking lot in the strip mall with a vacuum that needs to be repaired, our guy runs out and carries it in. That is consistent."

When we told Oreck during our conversation of our involvement and enthusiasm with and for the Entrepreneurs' Organization, formerly known as the Young Entrepreneurs' Organization or YEO, he suggested the proceeds for his charity designation related to this book go to this group, which inspires and supports entrepreneurs globally. More information can be found at www.eonetwork.org.

> **This genuine concern for people and giving back is a distinctly unique corporate attribute. This makes it clear why and how we say that these entrepreneurs create *authentic* brands.**

He closed with an anecdote that not only relates to authenticity—the theme of this book—but also seems to sum up his whole philosophy of doing good to do well. "People are always saying that they like our products," he smiled. "I had a woman stop me in the parking lot the other day. She had just been to our store, and she mentioned the address. She said 'I wanted to tell you, they were so nice to me.' It's a simple thing, just being nice to somebody."

This genuine concern for people and giving back is a distinctly unique corporate attribute. This makes it clear why and how we say that these entrepreneurs create *authentic* brands.

We cannot stress too much that doing good means doing well. The entrepreneurs interviewed for this book agree with this spirit of giving back and doing it from a place of concern and compassion.

Among the eleven charities named by the entrepreneurs to receive a portion of the proceeds from the sale of this book, Gary Hirshberg's donation will go to Clean Air Cool Planet (www.cleanair-cool-planet.org), and David Neeleman's to the JetBlue Crewmember Crisis Fund, and the Entrepreneurs' Organization.

Chapter 3:
Speak to Your Customers' Intelligence

Commitment to authenticity in dealing with customers is another common thread that connects the entrepreneurs with whom we spoke when developing this book. As demonstrated by strong mission statements that transcend their internal communications to reach their target audiences, most, if not all, of these business leaders have connected emotionally with their customers. This has occurred not only through effective marketing and public relations programs, but also through a non-adversarial, respect-based approach.

By emotionalizing their brands and producing exceptional quality not commonly found in competitive products and services, these entrepreneurs have created loyal and enthusiastic consumer bases.

Today's consumer, like today's businessperson, is more perceptive, skeptical, street-smart, and savvy than ever before. To thrive in this highly competitive business landscape requires being different. Authenticity requires addressing your audiences on their own level and having their best interests at heart, whether they are internal, including employees, or external, such as potential and existing customers, or business partners.

Jim Koch, creator of the Samuel Adams brand, has a particu-

> *As we will see in this chapter, authenticity in customer relations boils down to four cardinal rules:*
>
> 1. You must offer a genuine advantage to your customers or consumers.
> 2. Your marketing messages must be real, customer-centric, and must add value to the product or service being offered.
> 3. Your sales and distribution team must relay these key differentiators.
> 4. You must stand behind your product and keep your brand promise.

larly succinct way of looking at the authenticity of his relationship with his customers. "When I recall starting Sam Adams, one of the reasons I did it was that I wanted to have beer that I liked to drink, and nobody else was making it," he explains. "So it was *really* easy to identify with my consumers because *I* was the first one!"

How can you be more real about standing behind your product than that?

We have found that today's successful entrepreneurs take the needs and wants of their customers seriously. They don't speak down to them, but rather speak to them on their level. Connecting with the customers is the cornerstone of building brand loyalty and a brand following.

At JetBlue, the connection with customers comes from within, growing organically from a perception of the values by which the company's personnel conduct business. These values, as David Neeleman explained to us, are safety, caring, fun, integrity, and passion.

As Gary Hirshberg of Stonyfield Farm told us, "We've tried to be human, not talk in platitudes to our customers. We try to communicate our value system in a way that's humorous, a way that is light, and digestible. The whole idea of being human is not complicated for us, but it seems to be complicated for others to think that way. You just have to allow yourself to follow your instincts, not live in fear of the consumer but respect the consumers' judgment. You have to trust that if you are telling them sensible things, they will respect you."

An important part of this, as Hirshberg went on to explain, is to have a quality product and to have confidence in that quality. "Superior quality is a prerequisite to even entering the game. By definition, an entrepreneur is undercapitalized relative to the status quo. Therefore, if you enter a product category with a product that is either at parity with the leaders, or not as good, you won't even get to the starting line. If our yogurt wasn't better than the competition, nothing else would be relevant."

Of course, having the superior product or service leading the way is only the first step. You have to get it to your consumer. As we have already heard Gary Hirshberg joke, "We can ship our yogurt 3,000 miles, but it's the last 18 inches that make all the difference—getting that spoon to the customer's mouth!"

As with most entrepreneurs, Gary Hirshberg finds the Internet an important medium for communicating with Stonyfield's customers. "We use our packaging to send people to our website," he told us. "Here, we can have a deeper conversation about the issues that are important to us and to our consumers. We are trying to deliver on the promise that we are trying to help people as a solutions company. We deliver on that, in part, through our website. Here we have the opportunity to really deliver on who we are. We don't just go out and say we stand for this or that. We actually give people access to ways that they can find stuff. We have about 700,000 consumers who have actually subscribed to one of our four online newsletters with all the news that's fit to print. We have over 300,000 unique visitors every month and they stay an average of over five minutes, which is virtually unheard of. We know that other companies would kill for this kind of 'stickiness.'"

Jim Koch agrees that entrepreneurs have to be authentic in their approach to customers. For him, it begins with the sales person. "You're looking for somebody who takes initiative, has a high need for social interaction, low patience, low need for structure and order, and who understands the mission of service to the customer."

David Oreck, like Gary Hirshberg, feels that speaking to your customers' intelligence begins with making a good product. "Because it's a good product," Oreck told us, "we guarantee it longer than anybody else and agree to service it longer than others do. That type of customer service is getting harder to find. When you go into a department store to buy something, first you have to find someone to take your money, and a lot of people working in stores act as if the customer is bothering them. Apart from the ethical aspect of it, I think that treating the customer well, and doing things honestly, are just plain good business."

As with David Oreck and many other entrepreneurs with whom we've spoken, Starbucks founder Jerry Baldwin strongly believes that having a superior product is the first step toward consumer satisfaction. "At the head of the hierarchy of values that we established, was top quality coffee and tea, and a good work environment."

A good work environment is *authentic*, and this translates into both superior service and an exceptional customer experience, which clearly exude authenticity.

While he sees customer service as a key concept, Baldwin also views a good work environment as a prerequisite. "A good work environment and taking care of your people are what would lead to good customer service," he says. "With that hierarchy of values in place, next come social environmental concerns, which are now part of nearly any company's relationship with its customers and its community."

We asked Baldwin how important sampling the product was to establishing a connection with the customer. "It's important," he said. "I think guided sampling is much more important than just sampling. If you can engage in a conversation while the sampling is going on, you give the taster some factoids to hang the taste on. This way, you begin to establish the connection. In the case of coffee, staff knowledge really helps to create a customer connection."

While this creates a memorable connection with the consumer, ethnographic research goes even more deeply, studying and learning about consumer needs, cultural wants, and desires so that a company can better understand its customers and achieve a genuine connection.

He went on to say, "We tried to aim the business and the communication toward the most sophisticated observers and trend-setters. We figured that other people would follow. If you aim for the middle, if you think about the bell-shaped curve, you're going to get a much bigger potential market, but it would be a different business."

And, we might add, *not* necessarily an authentic experience.

For Jerry Baldwin, as with many others, customer service and social concerns are an essential part of the core values of successful, modern companies.

"This is certainly the case with Ben & Jerry's and Stonyfield Farm, as well as with Peet's, at least in our ownership of it," Baldwin explained, referencing his fellow entrepreneurs and his own work after leaving Starbucks. "The work that we did had nothing to do with 'branding and positioning;' it had to do with *the way we think*."

Ben Cohen and Jerry Greenfield are indeed considered leaders in elevating these core values to prominence within the context of a consumer-oriented business. "Ben and Jerry did things their way because that's what they believed," Baldwin noted. "For a lot of us who are about the same age, we grew up with this. For most of us, the traditional view of 'business' was something weird, but we redefined ourselves by redefining business. In school and thereafter we didn't think about it, except to the extent that you have to have a job so you can eat. Nobody wanted to be in 'business.' We were writers, artists, movie makers, and musicians—that sort of thing. Then all of a sudden, we woke up one day and said, 'Oh, we actually are in business,' instead of just making coffee or ice cream. It was quite a revelation."

Jerry Greenfield credited his partner for developing a very effective program of "relationship marketing."

"Whether it was special events or whatever, we wanted to have a relationship with our customers," Greenfield explained. "It's what Ben describes as an 'honest mission' that was *genuine*. We were a small business made up of real people. We thought that relationship-building and public relations rather than working through traditional advertising—which in the beginning we couldn't afford—was the best way for us to communicate. Relationship-building meant being actively involved in communities. We'd go out and serve ice cream and put on special events."

Of Alfred Peet, Jerry Baldwin said, "Hooking up with him early on was one of the things that we got right. Our having the benefit of his knowledge and his perceptions and his ability to distinguish quality, along with his ideas about relationships with customers, was crucial in forming ours at Starbucks."

Among his influences, Baldwin also cites Waverly Root, the visionary early twentieth-century food writer and journalist who lived in Europe during the 1930s, and who wrote such books as *The Food of France*, *The Food of Italy*, and *Food: An Authoritative and Visual History and Dictionary of the Foods of the World*, and Richard De Rochemont, who wrote *Eating in America: A History*. Root looked at food from the perspective that consumers responded more to subtlety than to hard sell.

"In *The Food of Italy*, Root describes Florentine cooking as paying careful attention to the selection of raw ingredients of the highest quality," Baldwin says. "Then he continues to describe 'cooking them with a minimum of sauces and seasoning. It's spare home cooking. Hearty and healthy, it's subtle in its deliberative eschewing of sophistication, which is perhaps the highest sophistication of all.' Ever since I read this book, this notion has guided me: Simplicity is the most sophisticated form of eating—and communication."

Keeping this sophisticated subtlety in mind, Baldwin recalls that one of his original Starbucks partners, Gordon Bowker, once said that "All coffee companies claim to have high-quality and fresh products, and to do the same is to reduce ourselves to their level."

Therefore, the Starbucks team countered with the notion

> "If one just takes a broader view, then the *customer* gets something, the *community* gets something, the *employees* get something, then the *company* makes money; and in a way we're all working together for mutual benefit."
>
> — Jerry Baldwin

that "if you have to claim it, you don't have it." From this concept, Starbucks applied the dictum "Show, don't tell." As Baldwin puts it, "Show your customers that you have good quality by actually delivering fresh coffee and tea. Intelligent people are active recipients of information, and they prefer to reach conclusions by themselves."

When it comes to the complex relationship between a company and its customers, Baldwin cites the work of the eminent Harvard sociobiology and biodiversity theorist Edward Osborne Wilson. He coined the phrase "scientific humanism" as being "the only world view compatible with science's growing knowledge of the real world and the laws of nature." His influential 1998 book, *Consilience: The Unity of Knowledge*, examines means that might be used to unite the sciences and which could one day combine the sciences with the humanities. Wilson chose the term "consilience" to characterize the synthesis of knowledge from various specialties and fields. He defines it as "literally a jumping together of knowledge by the linking of facts and fact-based theory across disciplines to create a common groundwork for explanation."

Jerry Baldwin told us, "Wilson has a lot of finely tuned arguments, but what really fascinates me is that he has advanced the idea that ethical behavior and morality have a genetic root. It always made sense to me that the longer version of the relationships with our customers is our relationships with communities. I believe strongly that the community, customers, vendors, and employees all could get something out of a corporation. Until the 1960s, and even later, it was a common idea that the corporation should just make money, making it a shareholder value thing. But I think that, if one just takes a broader view, then the *customer* gets something, the *community* gets something, the *employees* get something, then the *company* makes money; and in a way we're all working together for mutual benefit. This brings you to win-win rather than win-lose. To me, ethics is just a common-sense way of relating to people rather than something that has to do with religion."

When we asked Baldwin about leading, directing, and managing employees with regard to customer interaction, he explained, "Unlike quality management, customer-service management should *not* be hierarchical. Customer service needs to be participatory. Each person on the sales floor needs to be able to take care of the customer at that moment—not only to have the *authority*, but also the *responsibility*, to do it. He or she shouldn't have to say 'Gee, I've got to go talk to the manager about this.' "

This means that speaking to your audiences in an intelligent fashion includes speaking to the people within your organization that way as well.

The Authentic Brand

Chapter 4:
"Geo-Branding"

In developing their authentic brands and creating sustainable awareness, brand loyalty, and prominence in the minds of their customers, many of the entrepreneurial business leaders we interviewed closely linked themselves with their hometowns or states. One of the most important aspects of brand-building for small and regional businesses who plan to build their identity nationally is to "own their region."

Building a regional identity helps your brand's story resonate within that region and beyond. In turn, this leads to creating the image that you are *the* brand in your area. This is the process that we refer to as "Geo-Branding."

Without question, regional identity can be expanded to a national brand appeal. The local connection is powerful because the brands that originate and radiate from there are like a pebble dropped into calm waters. The rings can spread as

Building a regional identity helps your brand's story resonate within that region and beyond. In turn, this leads to creating the image that you are *the* brand in your area.

awareness and new brand fans are created. This is achieved through such building blocks as word-of-mouth, improved distribution, smart, emotionally stimulating packaging, sampling, and in blogs and communities on the Internet. Moreover, grassroots public relations, through its influential third-party endorsements, delivers high-impact media exposure that can generate consumer demand, or pull-through.

"The key to growing a business is that you need to be meeting some segment of the consumer's needs," Ben Cohen explains. "If you've got a small business and a product or service that is *not* popular, you simply have to *change* your product or service to be more popular. If you have a small business and the product or service is quite popular, and you're selling as much as you can make in a smaller geographic area, then your business is one that's ready to grow larger. Just don't grow any faster than you can develop good managers. You have to keep it authentic."

Entrepreneurs who have practiced Geo-Branding have benefitted from the intrinsic, positive associations of a geographic locale. By owning a territory, these innovators automatically created something real—not only by connecting with real places, but also with the feelings and associations people have with those places— *whether or not they've been there!*

In 1978, Ben Cohen and Jerry Greenfield started serving homemade ice cream out of a converted gas station in Burlington, Vermont. Within a very short time, by creating a homespun and amusing image, they had built the Ben & Jerry's brand into the signature ice cream of Vermont. Soon, they "owned" the ice cream market in New England, and they later became a national phenomenon. It wasn't just ice cream; it was a story about two guys who created stories behind every brand, from Chunky Monkey to Cherry Garcia.

Maine is one state that consistently spawns nationally beloved, smart brands. It is perceived as being a clean, genuine, down-to-earth place that is the ideal origin for natural products—especially water. Even if you have never been to Maine, you can imagine open spaces and natural goodness.

Take for instance, Burt's Bees, which Roxanne Quimby established as a ubiquitous brand in this lightly populated state before taking the brand national. Another example is Tom's of Maine. The company was founded by Tom and Kate Chappell in 1970 with just $5,000. Their mission was to

Entrepreneurs who have practiced Geo-Branding have benefitted from the intrinsic, positive associations of a geographic locale. By owning a territory, these innovators automatically created something real—not only by connecting with real places, but also with the feelings and associations people have with those places—*whether or not they've been there!*

make toothpaste and other personal-care products, made without artificial or animal ingredients and without using animal testing. Today, Tom's products are sold at more than 40,000 retail outlets worldwide. Their fluoride toothpastes are the only natural alternatives to earn the American Dental Association's Seal of Acceptance. Though Tom's of Maine was acquired by Colgate-Palmolive for $100 million in 2006, the previous owners retained a 16-percent share in the company, which remained based in Kennebunk, Maine. Under the terms of the deal, the original, authentic Tom's

Geo-Branding emotionalizes the brand and bonds people to it through helping them connect to the place and to a perceived way of life.

of Maine's policies were retained.

Also from Maine, but with a strong regional following throughout the Northeast, is Poland Spring Brand Natural Spring Water. Now a subsidiary of Nestlé, the company was founded in 1845. Poland Spring's water originates from multiple sources in the state, including Garden Spring and Poland Spring in Poland, Clear Spring in Hollis, Evergreen Spring in Fryeburg, Spruce Spring in Pierce Pond Township, and White Cedar Spring in Dallas, Maine.

The products of Ben & Jerry's, as well as those of Burt, Tom, and Poland Spring are consumed—often ravenously—well outside the geographic boundaries of Maine and Vermont. Geo-Branding emotionalizes the brand and bonds people to it through helping them connect to the place and to a perceived way of life. Vermont, for instance, emotes a clean, pure, simple, natural, genuinely good feeling. While this is a generalization, you get the point.

Jim Koch's Sam Adams brand resonated in the Boston area, and soon he "owned" the beer market in Beantown. This gave him the platform from which to launch his Samuel Adams product nationally. Another regional brewing company that had a passionate regional following before going national is Adolph Coors in Golden, Colorado. Before it established a nationwide distribution system, Coors had such a reputation that consumers often made buying trips to Colorado from states where the highly-prized beer was not available. The plot of the 1977 movie *Smoky and the Bandit* involved the "smuggling" of a shipment of Coors from Texas to

Georgia. Thanks to its being a Colorado-centric brand, Coors was the third largest brewing company in the United States during the 1970s, even though it was only a regionally distributed product. Since the late 1980s, with national distribution, it has maintained a position as a top-three brewer.

Today, another good example of a brewing company in the Mountain West that "owns" a market is Big Sky Brewing of Missoula, Montana. From its humble, albeit very authentic, beginnings in 1995, Big Sky has gone on to become the signature beer in Montana.

When it comes to "owning a territory" there are few better examples than the case of the man who, with our help, branded a Christmas tree in Oregon, a state where Christmas trees are a signature crop! Our firm came up with a strategy and created the world's first *real* "designer" Christmas tree, Oregon's Noble Vintage trees, grown by Joe Sharp's Yule Tree Farms in Oregon's renowned wine country, the Willamette Valley.

Sharp also recently introduced a live version of his Oregon's Noble Vintage trees. These trees have a tight, self-contained root system that settles in the earth immediately upon planting. A unique soil "recipe" of pumice and compost, as well as fine and coarse bark, also makes these trees lighter than a normal tree, allowing easy transport and handling. In a recent interview with William McCall of the Associated Press, Sharp explained that he has never found a better Christmas tree than in Oregon.

"It sounds gimmicky—and it kind of is—but it's working," wrote Elise Soukup in *Newsweek*. "While the rest of the national evergreen industry is hurting, as people turn to artificial varieties, Oregon's Noble Vintage sales have nearly doubled since they debuted last year, largely through word-of-mouth.... The trees, which are culled from the top ten percent of the crop, are valued for their symmetrical shape, vibrant color, long-lasting needles and, of course, the 'designer' moniker (prominently displayed on each tree's hang tag). They're especially popular in homes on a holiday house tour because, much like a designer handbag, the Oregon's Noble Vintage (which looks like a more perfect version of your off-brand tree) can be recognized by those in the know." Sharp delivers his live trees directly to consumers from his Internet site www.christmastreeoregon.com to anywhere in the United States.

The numbers of those "in the know" have increased dramatically since the trees have garnered extensive media coverage, including a mention on NBC's *The Today Show* and a story on the *History Channel*.

Gary Hirshberg of Stonyfield Farm began modestly in New Hampshire and went on to "own" that market for his yogurt brands before going national. Founded in 1983 as an organic farming school, Stonyfield Farm began with a few Jersey cows and a yogurt recipe. In the ensuing years, Hirshberg has built it into a $300-plus million-dollar company and the number-three yogurt brand in the world.

Stonyfield executed a smart Geo-Branding campaign using its New Hampshire farming roots, infusing and communicating a special and authentic element to the brand.

Today, Stonyfield Farm products, which include all-natural and certified-organic yogurt, smoothies, cultured soy, frozen yogurt, ice cream, and milk, are sold across the United States. Speaking from experience, Hirshberg has some cautionary words about the transition from a regional to a national brand: "Saying that your energy is best spent getting your product out in the test market doesn't mean you have to go national when you launch a product," Gary cautioned. "My counsel to entrepreneurs is to 'own' a region, 'own' a market, 'own' a segment, 'own' something. Create something you can defend. Don't get hung up on the idea that you have to go national instantly."

Hirshberg's advice also pertains to national companies that want to go global. Get it right here first—then expand overseas. His success and business practices have been so strategic, smart, and inspirational (while maintaining genuine concern for our planet) that Stonyfield's pure motives resonate with all who have experienced the brand—even their competitors.

It is no coincidence these companies have not only Geo-Branded themselves but, as an integral component of their marketing and business plans, they've also become involved with local causes. In Stonyfield's case, Hirshberg has genuinely and wholeheartedly embraced environmental and childhood-nutrition issues, which we discussed at length in Chapter 2.

Some people have even done such a good job of identifying with a territory that people across the nation think of them as *their* local brand. Wally Amos executed so many media events and traveled the country so often promoting Famous Amos Cookies that people thought he was from *their* hometowns. We have heard literally dozens of people swear that Amos was from Philadelphia, Los Angeles, Hawaii, New York, Chicago, or the District of Columbia. In fact, he was from Tallahassee, Florida. He just traveled so much doing national media tours that people believed he was their very own. And, we cannot neglect to remark that Starbucks is intrinsically associated with its Seattle base—yet another similarity found among our entrepreneurs.

The Authentic Brand

Chapter 5:
Story-Telling Creates Bigger Brands

Stories can form a strong emotional connection between a consumer and a product or service. This method of connectivity creates messages that are remembered, and brand recall translates as brand loyalty. In our public relations practice, we advocate creating a "brand personality," but through *authentic* stories about real people and companies.

When a talent agent named Wally Amos, formerly with the William Morris Agency, started a cookie company, promoting the cookie as he did the musical acts that he represented, he gave the new company a persona and created a captivating and *true* story around it. In our contemporary society, which is shaped by the entertainment industry, this insightful, authentic, and progressive marketing strategy eventually sparked a trend among food companies—and later thousands of consumer-product companies, from custom motorcycles to beauty products. Today, many successful brands utilize this strategy, which includes telling an interesting, memorable, and authentic story.

Consumers react positively to stories of real people who stand behind their brands. Orville Redenbacher, the botanist and businessman who created the popcorn that bears his name, was one,

> We advocate creating a "brand personality," but through *authentic* stories about real people and companies.

and so too was Colonel Harland Sanders, the founder of Kentucky Fried Chicken (KFC). Another excellent example of a businessperson who became his own spokesman and who developed an extraordinarily positive relationship with consumers was Dave Thomas. The founder and chief executive officer of Wendy's Old Fashioned Hamburgers, he is known for having appeared personally in more than 600 commercials for his restaurant chain, more than any other person in television history. And who can forget Victor Kiam, the president of Remington Products, the maker of razors and small appliances? Kiam appeared in ads for Remington razors saying that "I liked it so much, I bought the company!"

Meanwhile, the use of well-known celebrities, such as sports figures, with no integral connection with the company or product often backfires, particularly when they endorse several products, which consumers recognize and resent. A classic case is that of Hertz using a record-setting football player who won the Heisman Trophy as a running back for the University of Southern California, and who later played with the Buffalo Bills. His name was O.J. Simpson. He was a paid endorser who had nothing whatsoever to do with Hertz as a company. Professional public speakers often use this manipulation technique as well, though often with fabricated, unauthentic stories.

Other examples of *faux* spokespersons who are in stark contrast to Harland Sanders or Wally Amos are people such as Betty Crocker, the fictional female spokesmodel created in 1921 by the

Washburn Crosby Company (later General Mills) to answer mail that they received about baking with Gold Medal Flour, and Aunt Jemima, the fictional woman with a big smile who began promoting the products of the Davis Milling Company in the 1890s.

While many people still believe that Betty Crocker and Aunt Jemima were actually real, other companies have chosen spokesmodels that are more easily identified as fictitious. These range from the Campbell Soup Kids and the Chicken of the Sea Mermaid, to the Jolly Green Giant, Mr. Clean, and Ronald McDonald.

There was also the lonely Maytag Repairman, who appeared in countless television commercials between 1967 and 1988. He was actually an actor named Jesse White who was hired by the Leo Burnett Advertising Agency in Chicago. And who can forget Mr. Whipple, the persnickety storekeeper who admonished ladies not to squeeze the Charmin' toilet paper from 1965 to 1989? In a 1979 poll, Mr. Whipple was the third most recognized man in America, but that wasn't even his own name or identity. In fact, Mr. Whipple was really actor Dick Wilson—who earned a spot in the *Guinness Book of Records* for the longest commercial run in history—who had nothing to do with the product or the company.

While these characters captured the attention of consumers at a time when television commercials were viewed as genuine representations of reality, today's smart, ultra-busy consumer views television advertising with a healthy dose of skepticism—a compelling reason to create and develop more genuine spokespersons and brands.

Characters such as Dave Thomas and Wally Amos are much more compelling, because they have both charming personalities and stories that really *are* authentic. When Wally Amos founded his chocolate chip cookie brand and became "Famous" Amos, he actually baked the cookies.

"I didn't create my story," Wally Amos explained. "It's a *true story*. I started the cookie company. I *was* Famous Amos. The story was how I started the company. The story was my life and my belief system. I was the story. It's the same with my current Chip and Cookie brand. I'm not creating a story. The story is there. You live the story. When it's authentic, no one can dispute, deny, or steal it. You can't steal my personality or my enthusiasm. So when you *are* the story, I think you're head and shoulders above everyone else. *You* can't be Wally Amos. I'm the spokesperson for whatever it is that I do. Everybody is a spokesperson for what he or she does."

Amos points out that, when a story is contrived, "People see through it so quickly."

He also is quick to note that not every business has someone whom it can put forward as an authentic spokesperson for its products. "If you're fortunate enough to have someone to represent the brand, integrity, and the values of a company, I think it's a plus," he told us. "I think a spokesperson is very important, but everybody can't be a spokesperson."

In the course of interviewing the people whom we selected for this book, it became apparent that each of them had a compelling story, and that these stories have become an integral part of their brand identity.

As discussed in Chapter 1, when Roxanne Quimby met Burt Shavitz in the early 1980s, he was an unassuming beekeeper living on a small farm near Garland, Maine, and Roxanne was working three waitress jobs—and buying and selling at flea markets—to get by. She observed that Burt was selling his honey, but stockpiling his beeswax, so she suggested that he start making candles, and soon they were making beeswax lip balm. The immensely successful Burt's Bees line of natural personal-care products was born.

When we asked Gary Hirshberg of Stonyfield Farm how important a story is in marketing and in connecting with customers, he said succinctly that "It's everything."

He went on to say, "At Stonyfield Farm, we try to be human, and that begins with the way we tell our story. We don't try to pretend we are something we're not. We try to be sure that people understand our humble roots—and they are humble indeed. We started without a nickel in our pocket and seven cows."

He cites the recent popularity of "reality television" as an example of a consumer craving for authenticity. "I think people are starving to connect to the real thing," he said. "I think people want to believe, to have something they can believe in. I think that they want to know that dreams can come true. And of course, Stonyfield is a dream come true, so we fit into that pretty well."

When we asked him to relate the story of the humble roots and the dream that came true, he responded, "The question of how we got through those early years is really, really relevant. The short answer to a long question is that we begged, borrowed, and stole everything we could. By the early 1990s, we had over 300 individual shareholders, but not a single *institutional* one. It was a very lonely and hard time, but it gets me back to Nelson Mandela. I do know now from personal experience as well as his inspiration that you can triumph over any kind of adversity, and get through anything."

Gary Hirshberg went on to explain that he spends a huge amount of his time relating the Stonyfield Farm story to MBA

> **"If you're going to say something at all about your product, then it's better to have a story, especially an *authentic* one and an interesting one."**
>
> **— Jerry Baldwin**

students and entrepreneurs. In fact, he has set up the Stonyfield Entrepreneurship Institute, an annual boot camp where entrepreneurs can come to share stories.

"I spent nearly, no exaggeration, 90 percent of my time raising capital," he says of Stonyfield's formative years, relating tales that are all too familiar to entrepreneurs. "We used to joke that everybody with a necktie was fair game. I spent all my time with suits. We were fortunate in being able to identify ourselves with, and enable, some visionary, true-blue angels to stick with us through some really horrifically dark times. This included a year where we lost $1.4 million on sales of $2.5 million. I would wake up on Thursday mornings for 50 weeks in a row having to face our payroll with absolutely no idea where the money was coming from that afternoon. This was how we lived. Where did it come from? There are two answers. One is that we found the angels. The other is family, friends, and an unbelievable spouse."

"If you're going to say something at all about your product, then it's better to have a story, especially an *authentic* one and an interesting one," Jerry Baldwin, one of the original Starbucks partners, told us, reflecting on the importance of a story in crafting the image of a business. "The stories [of Starbucks] go back to how we found sources of coffee and tea, or stories from those countries. At first we felt we had to evoke European references to establish credibility. I think that even in our business, which is really based on taste and pleasure, it's helpful to have something to hang this taste memory on. It's helpful in 'emotionalizing' the connection with the product."

Many companies achieve authenticity by striving to have the best product available in a given sector. Orville Redenbacher's Gourmet Popping Corn became legendary for being significantly better than Brand X popcorn. Another good example is Eggland's Best eggs, which states that "Our goal is to have the freshest eggs possible in the supermarket." Eggland's Best eggs, whom our public relations firm represented for more than six years, are produced throughout the United States and are locally delivered fresh to the supermarket. Those years were a monumental time in the brand's history, achieving over 110 consecutive months of double-digit sales growth.

FoodReference.com has said, "Eggland's Best offers better taste, better nutrition, and better eggs. Specifically, Eggland's Best contain less saturated fat and lower cholesterol than ordinary eggs." They are also higher in Omega-3 fatty acids, lutein, vitamin E, and iodine. They are genuinely "good" eggs.

Stories don't usually get too much better than that, but this one does. It is also noted that, not only does FoodReference.com's chef use Eggland's Best eggs when testing recipes, but he also uses them at home too!

Jeff Taylor of Monster.com believes that, while stories have validity, they are meaningless without the company's itself being worthy of them. "I think that, in order to make the story relevant, your *company* has to be relevant," he told us. "You can make up stories about some old guy who did this or that, and that's how

> "We started out more as a product-based business, which was the simple handbag and our retail store, and we've evolved it into a lifestyle business that has a whole world around it."
>
> — Andy Spade

his company got started, but if his company doesn't *do* anything, nobody cares about his story. It's pretty well known that I came up with the idea for Monster in a dream. I dreamt up an $800 million company that has 4,000 employees in 26 countries, and that has a brand people know across the world. I think this makes the story relevant."

"Our story is still being written," Andy Spade told us. "With Kate and me, there is a story that wasn't 'developed.' It's just the *truth*. It wasn't like a marketing team went in and said 'Here's a void in the market, let's now create a name, let's create a product, let's fill the space.'"

"The story is that there were two people who moved here from outside of New York," Spade explained. "They started in their living room with no money, like a lot of young companies do, and made a good product. We did it because Kate wanted to wear a handbag that didn't exist in the market. She made the bag and it turned out a lot of people were feeling the same thing she was feeling, which is a story that other people have too. I think that this story is something people can relate to."

For Kate and Andy Spade, the step beyond their story is the creation of a lifestyle. "I think that we created a world around a handbag when most people said that you had to be 'ready-to-wear' to do a lifestyle," Andy Spade points out. "The traditional wisdom was that you can't do it with a product like a handbag. We started out more as a product-based business, which was the simple handbag and our retail store, and we've evolved it into a lifestyle business that has a whole world around it."

Kate Spade continued to evolve and break new ground as she chose additions to the product line. The first category into which the company extended after the Kate Spade Bag, was paper.

Communications experts and speech writers have long understood the power of story-telling, and it is a wonder that it has just caught on with businesses since the last quarter of the twentieth century.

"I don't think this had ever been done," Andy Spade observed, reflecting on other designers who had started out with handbags. "Usually people go into shoes or belts. We obviously did go into shoes soon after, but we went into paper first because that was our passion. Part of our story is that we are usually driven by our passion, and not by the marketing models that have been created before us by other companies. I think we're also probably the first handbag company to get a fragrance license without doing clothing first. Prada and Gucci both went into fragrance, but that was after they had been doing apparel, and Coach is just now finally launching its fragrance line. We have an eyewear license, which makes more sense because it's an accessory. These are examples of how we've evolved, and how we've developed a lifestyle brand."

Communications experts and speech writers have long understood the power of story-telling, and it is a wonder that it has just caught on with businesses since the last quarter of the twentieth century. It finally has, and it has done so with the help of pioneers like Wally Amos, who also trail-blazed cause marketing at a time when most businesses hadn't considered the value of either. Marilyn and John Rosica and I feel honored to continue to work with him after all these years. We are presently working together promoting Uncle Wally's Muffins, which is highly successful and continues to grow and innovate.

Chapter 6:
Flying Under the Radar:
A Great Way to Crash and Burn

Through the years, we have met with and counseled countless CEOs, company presidents, entrepreneurs, marketing directors, and vice presidents, all of whom wanted to improve their businesses and gain a competitive advantage. Despite the fact that these bright, tenacious, success-driven professionals were meeting with us—public relations and marketing counselors (experts in creating *heightened* brand awareness)—many wanted to keep much of their success and businesses a *secret!*

For example, in the last several years, we have had meetings with a company that had an innovative method of retaining clients; another with a new manufacturing process that could transform the beauty industry; a software developer with a cutting-edge technology that could significantly impact the financial-services industry; a fitness-equipment maker with a clearly superior product line; and a food manufacturer with a new line of healthier snack foods.

When discussing their business and marketing goals, they each told us that they wanted to stay under the radar.

However, in all of these meetings, each of these real companies had one thing in common: When

> **"I think there's a big difference between knowing what the formula is and actually *executing* that formula. I'm a strong believer in the idea that you really dictate your own success. If you have a tremendous amount of confidence, the best team, and your execution is better than anyone else–bring it on!"**
> **—David Neeleman**

discussing their business and marketing goals, they each told us that they wanted to—and I quote—"*stay under the radar.*" This was despite the fact that each had unambiguous, newsworthy differentiators that set them apart from their competitors!

Despite the fact that these folks met with our public relations agency, whose sole mission is to disseminate a client's most compelling attributes, they were fearful that someone would steal their idea or try to knock them off. How can a brand or company be first or be perceived as best in a category by taking this stance? Or even more importantly, how can a brand be the preferred brand of choice if nobody knows about it?

It boggles the mind.

We certainly understand the genuine need to safeguard proprietary technologies, business practices, or inventions. As Jerry Baldwin puts it, "You don't want to get shot down. There are probably some businesses, especially in the tech field, where you want to get the product established and trademarked before the competition does. Coffee and tea are in the public domain. For us, execution is everything."

However, if a product or service is ready to be sold and a distribution plan is in place, why not get it out there and *own* a category in the minds of your potential customers?

Jim Koch is an example of one of those who was reticent to show the flag in the beginning. He feels that, when he began his Boston Beer Company in 1985, perceived competition from established national brands kept him under the radar initially. However, he did not remain there. By the mid-1990s, Samuel Adams was well above the radar, and one of the leading brands to have emerged from the craft-brewing movement of the previous decade. The brand had become a household name. Today the name "Samuel Adams" may be better known around the country as a brand of beer than as the eighteenth-century Boston patriot for whom his brand is named.

We asked David Neeleman of JetBlue how he would calm the fears of someone who was inclined to fly under the radar.

"I can go only by my own experience, and it would be pretty hard for me to consider flying under the radar. I'm very well aware that there are predatory competitors that are willing to do just about anything to knock you out of business. However, in the airline business, the most successful companies, such as Southwest Airlines, are quite open about what they are doing. Southwest's formula is no secret, but no one's been able to duplicate it. Then there's Dell, the computer company. There are so many people who want to be Dell, but they can't do it."

Neeleman is just the opposite of those whose inclination is to fly under the radar, because he sees the strategy as being just as unnecessary as it is counterproductive.

"I think there's a big difference between knowing what the formula is and actually *executing* that formula," he smiled. "I'm a strong believer in the idea that you really dictate your own success.

If you have a tremendous amount of confidence, the best team, and your execution is better than anyone else—bring it on!"

While others hide, Neeleman is always willing to disclose anything and everything about his customer-service practices, training programs, growth plans, and marketing tactics.

"I'm not one to hide what we're doing," he told us. "Obviously we hide where we're going to fly next for competitive reasons, but as far as our technology, we're pretty up front about it. We have actually shared our in-home reservation system with our competitors. They have come in and taken a look at what we do. We aren't afraid because we're confident that we can continue to do it better than they can."

You can worry only so much about what a competitor *might* do. Different people often have the same idea at the same time. Things just happen that way. One of the most memorable examples occurred on the morning of February 14, 1876, when Elisha Gray, an electrical engineer from Highland Park, Illinois, arrived at the U.S. Patent Office to register a patent for the telephone. Much to his surprise, he learned that Alexander Graham Bell had registered a patent for a telephone only a few hours earlier. Working independently, both Gray and Bell had each invented the telephone at almost exactly the same time.

It was Jerry Baldwin who pointed out how frequently this sort of thing occurs, albeit not in so dramatic a fashion as with the telephone.

"What's fascinating to me is how people who are unrelated in different parts of the country and the world, and who have no contact, will come up with the same idea at the same time," he observed. "In 1963, a coffee operation opened in Los Angeles.

Alfred Peet opened in 1966. We knew about one but not the other when we opened in 1971. Then somebody started in Seattle the same year we did. These things just kind of happened at the same time. It's like they sprang spontaneously out of the culture. Some of this is going on even in the tech field."

In the beginning, however, there was a tendency to shy away from advertising at Starbucks. "Beyond not hiring a publicist, we also didn't publicize ourselves too well back then," Jerry Baldwin recalls. "I used to say that we hid behind our product. I would much rather have seen a story about us on the feature page or the food page, rather than the business page. Coming from where we did, we didn't even read the business page. That was for old guys. But today, everybody reads the business page. Ever since the beginning of the 1990s, you don't care where you get the buzz as long as you get it somewhere."

Baldwin went on to say that an entrepreneur should think big, and shouldn't let fear of the competition hold him back. When Starbucks first thought about expanding from Seattle, the partners naturally considered Portland, because it was close.

"The more we thought about it, the more we asked ourselves why we should screw around with a market which then had half a million people, when there were six million in the San Francisco Bay Area," he says. "There were many different cities in the Bay Area and clearly more opportunity. Will the competition be stiffer? Of course it will, but, let's go. Fish where the fish are. It contrasted with the founders of Minneapolis-based Caribou Coffee, and other businesses that have said they want to stay out of Starbucks' way. I think it would have been better for them to go head to head into the stiff competition—rather than to go to secondary markets

> "People will much more believe what they read in a magazine article or quote than they will on an ad anyway."
>
> —Bobbi Brown

where there wasn't much business and therefore not much profit, even if you were successful."

We asked Gary Hirshberg, the chairman, president, and "CE-Yo" of Stonyfield Farm about whether "flying under the radar" was a sound business and marketing strategy for his company in the yogurt market—and his answer was a straightforward "No, *absolutely not!*"

He went on to elaborate, telling us that, in the twenty-first century, "This is no longer possible in consumer products. Thanks to Google, the speed of information, and the search engines, everything is known instantly. The energy you're going to spend trying to stay *under* the radar is better spent getting out there and testing your product."

Speaking of the fear of having a concept or idea knocked off, he insists that it is better to move forward, because in his words, "It is as much about execution as it is about content. The difference between doing it and thinking about doing it is everything."

The message here is that if you are different, do it right, engage employees and customers, and if you are authentic and original, by all means, tell the world about it.

Hirshberg goes on to give the example of O'Naturals, his organic and natural restaurant chain, which began modestly with a handful of locations in Maine and Massachusetts. "It is a better widget," he says enthusiastically. "The food is fantastic, and people love it. The repeat business is awesome and profitable. Candidly, every smart person I know has thought of this idea, so there is no ESP here. I don't lose sleep over whether somebody is going to come in and take photographs, which they do, or study it and steal ideas, which they do. You've got to hit it on the head. I do think that people who have a superior product—if it's truly superior—do themselves a disservice in thinking that someone else can just walk in and steal it. Of course, if it's not truly superior, then you shouldn't be doing it anyway."

To us, *true* superiority rings of authenticity.

"The desire to fly under the radar was never a problem for me, because I'm a public person," Wally Amos said as he told us about developing his new Chip and Cookie brand. "When I start a business, I want as much exposure as I can get. With Chip and Cookie, we're investing in public relations, which built the Famous Amos brand, and we're buying newspaper ads, as well as advertising time on radio and television stations. I want to hit the ground running. I think that public relations is very important. I think that exposure in a business is absolutely critical. It is important to let the public know you got a product!"

He shrugged off fears of being ripped off, saying, "I don't think anybody can take my idea. It can't be taken. I might share it with you, but what's mine is mine, because I'll do it my way, and different from someone else. I know that this kind of stuff goes on in people's lives and businesses, but that's not the way that I do business. That's not a part of my belief system. When I started Famous Amos, I knew that there would be other cookie companies. So what? None of them will have cookies that taste as good as mine, nor give it the heart and soul that I gave my cookies!"

Jeff Taylor of Monster.com recalls being very much *above* the

> **We are recurrently perplexed when we meet with a company that wants to compete on price alone. This is a surefire way to commoditize almost any product or service.**

radar when he started. You don't use a name like "Monster" without getting noticed!

Taylor recalls, "I've done crop circles outside of O'Hare Airport. I put blimps up in the sky for cigarette companies or beer companies when no traditional companies did that. Those kinds of things bring a brand to life. A lot of the marketing tools become stories around the brand that you create."

Taylor is not shy about pushing brand awareness. He cites the example of when Monster was a corporate sponsor of the Winter Olympics. "We built the largest snowman in the world right in the Olympic Village," he grinned. "At the end of the day it was the snowman and the public relations it generated that kind of defined our character. We spent $15 million being an Olympic sponsor, and the snowman cost $58,000. My point is that it's not just about the dollars, it's about the ideas, and about applying those ideas."

We found the same thing when we were branding Famous Amos. We did it on a shoestring budget, which is possible with the right strategy and an authentic offering.

Sometimes, smart entrepreneurs are perceived as flying further above the radar than they actually are—often with prodigious and larger-than-life results.

"I find it actually kind of bizarre and funny that people are always calling to interview me," Bobbi Brown laughed. "What did you eat for breakfast? Where did you go on the holiday? Where do you buy your clothes? Women come up to me and say 'Oh, I did that because you said…'. Once, a woman from some English magazine, *English Vogue* or something, phoned to ask me where I get my hair done. Instead of saying, 'Some fabulous salon,' I told her the truth, which was Joe Difranse at Esthetica Salon in Montclair, New Jersey. Well, she took the plane to New York and the car service to Esthetica. It really looked like a beauty salon a grandmother would go to before they renovated it. This poor woman was probably like, 'Oh my god.' That was very funny."

Getting serious, Bobbi Brown went on to say, "I know that a lot of women look up and relate to me because I am a woman, because I'm a mom, and because I have kids. I'm very honest, and always talk about issues that women have. I try to solve beauty problems with my products. I've written four books that are very self-esteem-driven. I'm on *The Today Show* once a month so they see me a lot, and I've learned in my business we are not a big advertising business, but we are a huge public relations business. People will much more believe what they read in a magazine article or quote than they will in an ad anyway. I'm lucky that I have a relationship with all the editors at the magazines and they are really supportive of things and naturally excited, so we get pretty good coverage, and I feel really fortunate."

Before selling her company in New York City, real-estate entrepreneur Barbara Corcoran told me a similar story. She said, "When I had four people working for me, I focused three quarters of my time on public relations, and I got a story in *The New York Times*. The perception was that I had 40 employees. When I had 40 people, I was in *The Wall Street Journal* and it seemed as though I had 400."

For her first several years in business, she dedicated the majority of her time to public relations, and she was the company's visible and credible spokesperson. She deliberately chose *not* to fly under the radar.

From our experience working with a wide array of product and service companies since 1980, it is clear that the ones that speak to their customers' intelligence—*and speak loudly*—are the ones that command a premium for the extraordinary value they deliver. In fact, we are recurrently perplexed when we meet with a company that wants to compete on price alone. This is a surefire way to commoditize almost any product or service and create a volatile trade environment, as many have found when competing for Wal-Mart's business: here today, gone tomorrow. There has to be some deep-seated reason *why* someone would want to do business with you. This *why* is directly connected with your key differentiators and adds value above and beyond the competition. Kate Spade, Ben and Jerry, Famous Amos, Starbucks, and several others we interviewed charge a premium for excellent quality and service—so price *does not have to be a factor.* Joe Gantz, a member of the World Presidents' Organization who served as my mentor several years ago, once told me, "If you compete on price, there will always be someone who will beat yours, so look to your strengths and focus on those." I never forgot his words, and I wrote them down in case I ever did.

While a more cautious entrepreneur may choose to lie low and "fly under the radar," the business leaders with whom we spoke took the high road, told the world about their companies, and disseminated their good news. As a result of putting their best face forward, they created successful companies and built significant brand equity.

The Authentic Brand

Chapter 7:
Leadership Qualities and Beliefs

I t seems intuitive to state categorically that every leader leads differently. It seems like common sense. Some, like David Oreck, are very hands-on, preferring to steer the ship and be involved in nearly every aspect of the business. Others surround themselves with key staff or partners from the beginning and rely on their expertise to grow the business. It is certainly true that leaders have differing styles, and we have clearly seen that in the men and women with whom we spoke while writing this book. However, certain common threads have emerged.

While they each welcome input from their people, these business builders don't make important decisions by consensus. They take responsibility for calling the shots that really matter. Each sets measurable benchmarks and goals for his or her company and people to ensure results. They personally hire key management based on personality in order to ensure that their mission and brand promise thrive.

In this chapter, we ask the entrepreneurs to define their own leadership styles and how they make key hiring decisions. We ask

These business builders don't make important decisions by consensus.

> **"If you're just there to make a quick buck and get out, or if you don't wake up in the morning thinking about it and go to bed at night thinking about it, then you're not an entrepreneur."**
>
> **—David Neeleman**

who influenced them, and how they felt about personal issues such as risk-taking and family involvement. We also ask them to reflect on ventures where they had failed, and how they pulled themselves back up by their bootstraps and moved on.

When looking at leadership style, we have discovered in our conversations that successful entrepreneurs are invariably *passionate* about their businesses. As David Neeleman said, "You need to be expressive, and you need to be passionate. One of the things you have to do as an entrepreneur is to be able to paint a picture in the minds of your investors and crew members and everyone else. I tell aspiring entrepreneurs that they have to be passionate about their business. You have to live it and breathe it. If you're just there to make a quick buck and get out, or if you don't wake up in the morning thinking about it and go to bed at night thinking about it, then you're *not an entrepreneur.* That's okay; you don't *have to* be an entrepreneur. If that's what you aspire to be, however, you won't be successful unless you're completely enthralled with the business."

Leadership Styles

In our conversations, as we asked the various entrepreneurs to reflect on their own leadership styles, most responded that it was a tough question because it is hard to define oneself. Having said that, they had a lot to tell us about how they saw themselves as leaders.

"People who work at JetBlue respect me and know that I'm the guy who is building the company on their backs," David Neeleman explained. "They know me as somebody who's really trying to strengthen a company instead of trying to make all the money and go buy himself a private jet and an island somewhere. They know me as somebody who is sharing and trying to work with them to build a company where people feel part of the organization. They know that their president is a guy who works for nothing, allows them to buy stock at a discount, shares the profits with them, provides good health care, and a competitive wage. Everyone, 100 percent of our people, gets profit-sharing checks if we make money in the year. In addition, 80-plus percent of our people are shareholders in the company because they can buy discounted company stock."

Moving into his personal management style, he told us: "I'm very tolerant of people who are working hard and doing their best, and very intolerant of people who are affecting either their fellow crew members or our customers in a negative way. I have a certain standard about which I feel very strongly that we need to uphold. I'm absolutely cool when everything's going the way that it should and people are working hard."

As with David Neeleman, Jerry Baldwin sees a great deal of value in having the whole team on the same page. "I believe there is great value in everybody's knowing what's going on," he told us. "What I hate to hear is the use of the pronoun 'they' by an employee. It's 'we,' not 'they.' To the extent that everyone is involved, it's 'we.' The whole army has to be going in the same direction."

Verne Harnish, the author of *Mastering the Rockefeller Habits* and the founder of the Entrepreneurs' Organization (formerly the Young Entrepreneurs' Organization), recommends daily huddles, or stand-up meetings, to enhance company or team communications. In our public relations business, we've seen this work extremely well to foster good internal communications.

In an article for a recent issue of *Fortune Small Business*, Harnish wrote, "What makes a quarterly goal achievable is a daily and weekly rhythm aimed at keeping everyone informed, aligned, and accountable…. One of the most successful practices any company can implement is that of a daily huddle—no more than 15 minutes per group, in a room or on a daily conference call, just to celebrate progress or identify barriers blocking that progress. The great petroleum tycoon John D. Rockefeller held such a meeting with his executives every day of the 19 years he spent building Standard Oil. The meeting not only keeps people informed but also helps put out fires that could burn up time at the weekly meeting, where the main topic should be the quarterly goals."

Reflecting upon the role of the entrepreneur both as the person in charge, and as a part of the "we" of the organization, Jerry Baldwin told us that he believes that good leaders must see themselves as a worker among workers—but first and foremost, they still have to direct, manage, and lead.

"At first, we looked at profit as not necessarily a good thing," he said. "The biggest revelation for us 'sixties' guys was to get the idea that a profitable, well-run business enabled us to do a lot of different things. The important thing is to understand that there is a lot of strength in seeing oneself as fundamentally the same as everybody else in the company. At the same time, it might get in the way of being a leader. Seeing that in the beginning is a very important thing.

"Taking a step away from myself, what I would say to these leaders is to tell them that people really want you to do your job," Baldwin continued. "That's what they really want. You get paid more than they do, they know who the boss is, and they expect you to lead. There might be some immature people who would say, 'Gee, cut me some slack and don't be the boss,' but in the end somebody has to organize and show direction. Unlike managing customer service, the management of quality should be hierarchical. We don't need a thousand people deciding how an espresso should be made. We need one person deciding how the espresso should be made, and you should make it that way every time."

He went on to compare the dynamics of teams within a company to that of a team playing on a court. "This hierarchical model is like football. The coach calls the play, and play stops all the time for people to regroup. That's fine for executing a singular view, but terrible for taking care of customers. Our model for customer service is like a basketball or soccer team. The play is constant, so the coach can't intervene. Each player must know his or her role, and all the players must be able to trust each other's competence and judgement. If everyone is where he or she belongs, you don't have to look before you pass. You just know. Take care of your customer; don't look to the coach."

We asked whether this could be applied to all aspects of the business, causing it to cease to be participatory.

"I think people are intelligent," Baldwin explained. "The staffs that we hire are smart. I've rarely met someone who didn't want to do a good job. So a manager's job is to provide an atmosphere where somebody can succeed."

When we asked about how he would describe his own managerial style, he said: "I probably drive people crazy with requests for more information and more numbers, but I have the ability to look at a set of numbers and see the anomalies jump out. I always want more information, but that forms the basis for communicating. Personally, I'm actually kind of shy, but I'm comfortable out in public. I'm a little reticent at first when I'm approaching people, but once I get going, I'm expressive."

Jim Koch sees his own analytical style as having been forged by his having attended the Harvard Business School and spending six years with the Boston Consulting Group. He does not, however, see this as a hindrance to creativity. "To me, one can be both fact-based and analytical, *and* creative," he explained. "That's actually quite a useful combination. One is both able to come up with ideas and to filter out the 90 percent of them that are dumb. You are left with some that may wind up being a waste of time, but at least you did filter out the ineffective ones. I'm lucky, because I've done all the jobs within the company. I understand the different constraints. For example, there might be something that seems great, like a swing-top, but there's no way to make it work on our bottling line."

Bobbi Brown, meanwhile, thinks of herself as "the opposite of analytical."

"I'm incredibly expressive, open, and truthful," she told us. "I hate liars and I don't like to lie. If someone asks me 'Do you like my haircut?' I can't lie. I'll say 'No, I liked it better the other way, but don't worry, it'll grow.' My style is definitely verbal. I'll tell you exactly what I think."

In applying this principle to operations within the company, Bobbi told us that she doesn't like it when the creative teams spend a lot of time putting together a presentation that she may not like. She considers this a waste of time and would rather discuss an idea at its inception.

"Even if they've done a phenomenal job, I hate being presented to because usually that means that they've gone off and done all this work," she said. "I like to be a part of it. Probably to a fault, I get really excited about certain little things. I'm happy for people to take risks, but often a lot of time and money is wasted because it wasn't a direction that we wanted to go in."

As with Bobbi Brown, Gary Hirshberg readily defines himself as more expressive than analytical. "I'm a gut guy and I don't tend to trust data," he explained. "This is the greatest challenge that I pose to my people, who are, of course, professionals, and, in many cases, excellent analysts. Their reality stems from what they believe in the evidence that they've collected from consumer research, or from financial metrics. I'm an out-of-the-box guy. My job is to question whether there may be a different way to do something."

As our conversation turned to the notion of leadership, Hirshberg told us candidly, "I tend to lead by *inspiration*, but I suspect that I often lead by *frustration*. I'm fairly self-aware in that I *know* that I'm not an easy guy to be with or work with. As I've said, we're really in the business of invention here, so I take the risk that people's skin is thick enough to handle it. When you have somebody who drives you crazy, it pushes you to anticipate and betters your arguments."

"I've always viewed the vice presidents essentially as CEOs in their own areas," Hirshberg explained, elaborating on the structure of the company and his own hands-off style of management. "As long as they are delivering the numbers and the results we

> **"One of the ways I evaluate whether it's a good idea or not is to look at whether it just doesn't go away."**
> **—Jeff Taylor**

agreed on, I stay the hell out of their way."

Like many of the entrepreneurs in this book, Kate and Andy Spade like to be involved in the creative process. In our conversation with Andy, he defined himself as a collaborator. "I love collaborating, and I've worked with a lot of bright people inside and outside of the company," he told us. "It's not formalized at all. We borrow from everywhere and make decisions based on our gut instinct and a little bit of business sense. I have a point of view on things, but I'm very open-minded. By no means am I a micromanager or a dictator. I listen to other people's points of view and ask for better ideas. I try to hire good people who have better ideas."

While Spade calls himself a collaborator, David Oreck readily acknowledges, "I'm pretty domineering when it comes to business, although I am a good listener, and I *do* listen."

As we talked, Oreck shared his ideas on what it takes to be a good listener. "I think a lot of people don't listen," he said. "They're thinking about what they're going to say, not what the other guy is saying. They just wait for their chance to talk. The minute there's a silence in the conversation, they're in there. I like to feel that I'm a good listener, although I don't think I always was. I've found that two people can't be talking at the same time and, if your mouth is working, your ears aren't."

Jeff Taylor told us that he operates with what he modestly describes as "a naïve confidence."

"This is something that has developed through the course of my life," he explained. "It's an ability to take on big projects. I think a second thing is that I'm just really curious. I ask question after question after question. One of my discoveries is that if there is something that really interests me, I have both passion and direction. I have the passion to learn and the direction to go after it. These are attributes that have stayed with me pretty much through my adult life. And I think, by the way, that I really *developed* these in my adult life. I was a shy kid in junior high and high school, and I kind of came into my own in college. I really feel that I'm a late bloomer. Some people burn out or fade out too early, but I think I'm still trying to figure out how to bloom in my forties."

We followed up by asking Taylor how he applies this inquisitiveness to problem-solving. We've found many differences among entrepreneurs. Some people trust their own instincts and others discuss things before coming to a conclusion. We wanted to know whether he speaks with other people to come up with solutions or conclusions, or typically formulates them on his own after investigating a question.

"It's a combination," he told us. "I do both because, when I formulate an idea, one of the ways I evaluate whether it's a good idea or not is to look at whether it just *doesn't go away*. I've also trusted my own instincts really throughout the business process, in particular at Monster. It's the idea of the gut feel, the premonition, or the ability to be able to see things in your own mind."

Time Management

We've found that a good way to assess a leader's style is to ask how he or she evaluates a situation where there are numerous tasks to be

Entrepreneurs, business leaders, and managers have extremely busy schedules and multiple priorities, so it is easy to fall into the trap of doing things that are easier to complete first—because checking items off the list gives you a sense of accomplishment. While this is true, it is a tendency that must be addressed and overcome in order to achieve bigger and better things, as our interviewees have disciplined themselves to do.

addressed simultaneously. Which do you tackle first? If you have 20 things to do, and three of them are really hard and important, while the others are less so, do you try and knock off the 17 easier ones—or decide you can live with the smaller stuff and go after the three toughest things first?

"For me, it's all about the most important things," David Neeleman told us. "Prioritizing is very important. I think that being an entrepreneur is knowing what's important and what isn't. I don't do things that I don't think are important, and I try to do the things that I think *have the most impact on the company* and delegate other things to someone else. The hardest thing is knowing what has the biggest impact."

Jerry Baldwin agreed that knowing what has the biggest impact is both important and difficult. He observed that this is something that has to be learned, and it is not easy. "With the benefit of hindsight, I think the organization became much more professional over time and it happened organically. If one could wave a magic wand, the best thing would have been to have started out knowing what was most important to deal with first. Whether the company would be as strong is another question. The most important thing I would say is that, if you have something that requires long-term thinking, work on it early so that you don't end up at the deadline saying 'Oh, crap.'"

Jeff Taylor stresses the importance and the difficulty of knowing what to tackle first. "This is not my strongest point," he admitted. "I think that human nature is to work on what's the most fun, so I'm as guilty as the next person. Maybe the subtlety that's missed is that what is the most fun may *not* be what you're the best at. You need to be able to delegate things that you aren't as good at or things that aren't as fun, so you can take on more that will help you love your job."

As for the process of actually tackling a task, Taylor told us: "I think there's no time like the present. A lot of people get panicky about getting stuff done, but the way to get stuff done is to *get on the phone and get started with it*. I'm way too busy. I have two days worth of work within every single day, so I just continue to prioritize and re-prioritize and just don't give up."

Entrepreneurs, business leaders, and managers have extremely busy schedules and multiple priorities, so it is easy to fall into the trap of doing things that are easier to complete first—because checking items off the list gives you a sense of accomplishment. While this is true, it is a tendency that must be addressed and overcome in order to achieve bigger and better things, as our interviewees have disciplined themselves to do.

Wally Amos feels that, if he doesn't deal with those things that are top priority, and actually get them done that day, he won't accomplish his ultimate goals.

> **"All we can do is control the 'controllables.' There are lots of things that cannot be controlled, so why waste the energy?"**
> **—Wally Amos**

"You can't put it off," he told us. "You deal with those things that are top priority, not necessarily the hardest. One thing that stands out in my mind when I started Famous Amos is the night before a store-opening party. No one knew how to make cookies, so the night before the party I had to start making cookies. I decided that I was going to make chocolate chip with pecan and a butterscotch chip with pecan. I figured that I had better do the butterscotch chip with pecan first, because no one else knew what a butterscotch chip with pecan was. I figured that I'd get them out of the way, and then I'd work on the chocolate chip with pecan. Everybody has his or her own prioritizing ways. I tackle those things that most *need* to be done, not necessarily the more difficult things. That's where I put my energy and my time."

On the issue of time management and managing stress, Amos once remarked that a CEO friend of his who runs a Fortune 500 company said (and we paraphrase), "All we can do is control the 'controllables.' There are lots of things that cannot be controlled, so why waste the energy?"

David Oreck believes that a key to prioritization is avoiding procrastination. Like Wally Amos, he believes in doing it today rather than putting it off. One of the ways he stays on top of things is to address them immediately. "Time is not your friend, it is your enemy," he said. "In business, you've got to watch for the small things, because they frequently point to a problem that could be devastating."

Influences and Role Models

You can also learn a lot about a person's own leadership qualities and beliefs by asking him or her to name and describe people who have influenced and inspired him or her.

When we asked David Neeleman who in the business world had most influenced him,

> **"In business, you've got to watch for the small things, because they frequently point to a problem that could be devastating."**
>
> **—David Oreck**

he quickly mentioned his former employer, Herb Kelleher, the co-founder, chairman, and former CEO of Southwest Airlines. Having earned his law degree from New York University, Kelleher and one of his law clients, Texas businessman Rollin King, sketched out the idea that became Southwest on a cocktail napkin in a San Antonio restaurant. When it started in 1971, the airline broke new ground in the industry by offering low fares and operating through secondary, under used airports in major metropolitan areas, such as Midway in Chicago and Oakland.

"Herb Kelleher obviously is someone that I really look up to," Neeleman told us of a man who is now one of his main competitors. "It's pretty rare that you look up to someone who fired you, but I do. He has done an amazing job. To be able to withstand the test of three decades of profitability is just amazing in our industry. He's still a really good friend of mine, and he's someone I've really admired for what he's been able to do. I have patterned a lot of what JetBlue does after Southwest. I had the advantage of starting with a clean white piece of paper, so I think we do it better in a lot of areas, but I really admire what he's done."

On the personal side, David Neeleman told us that he was influenced by his father. "My dad really taught me to love people and to really value every single person. He was always a person who fought for the underdog. Even in sports, we always rooted for the team that was supposed to lose. The only time I ever heard him say something negative about anyone was about people who thought they were better than others."

Jim Koch credits his father as both a business and personal influence. Indeed, Charles Koch, himself a fifth-generation brewmaster, sits on the board at Jim's Boston Beer Company.

"My dad was a brewmaster, but he never owned a brewery," Jim explained. "The breweries he worked for were small, traditional breweries that were slowly going out of business. He was working for small breweries while they were being driven out by the mass-marketed beers. I saw how his career as a brewmaster had been, and I wanted to try to change that history and take the next step. I wanted to be the next turn of that cycle where the small breweries came back."

"I've been lucky enough to meet a lot of people over the years," Koch continued. "One person I've met only a couple of times, but whom I've always thought of as a role model, is Robert Mondavi. He did with American wine what I set out to do with American beer. By making great American beer, I wanted to change the way Americans thought about their own beer and their brewing, just as Robert Mondavi did. I thought, if I make great beer here in the United States, one of the ways I'll measure whether we've been successful is whether we're able to upgrade the opinion that Americans have of their own beer."

For Andy and Kate Spade, it was their mothers who were their biggest personal influences.

"Kate talks about her mother a lot," Andy Spade told us, "in terms of giving her the ability to create and accessorize individually. I can't think of any specific fashion-world business models that she has had."

As for Andy himself, he credits his own mother for her support: "She encouraged me to take risks and believe in myself, supporting me on that level."

Among the others whom Andy cites is branding and marketing guru Richard Kirshenbaum, the co-chairman of Kirshenbaum, Bond, and Partners, one of the largest creative advertising agencies in the country, as well as the author of *Closing the Deal* and *Under the Radar: Talking to Today's Cynical Consumer.*

"Kirshenbaum was my mentor for about five years," Andy explained. "He taught me how to be a gentleman and a business person at the same time."

Andy also goes on to credit advertising executive Jay Chiat, calling him "an innovative thinker who encouraged us to think in different ways and gave us confidence to solve problems in unexpected ways."

Jerry Greenfield also looked to his mother as an important influence. She had just passed away when we were talking to him for this book.

"My mother was just incredibly kind, and she was a thoughtful and caring person," Jerry explained. "She was always thinking about trying to help other people. When she was alive and doing it, I used to wonder, 'Boy, doesn't she have any interests of her own, or anything that she likes to do?' Finally, I came to realize that *this* was what gave her joy. It was helping other people out. It was a

> "Just because something hasn't been done this way before, it doesn't mean we shouldn't try it, or that it's not possible."
> —Jerry Greenfield

nice tribute to her ideals and selflessness when we were able to do these things as a business."

On the business side, Jerry told us that he and Ben Cohen entered the business without really having a specific role model, although they would discover role models later. In 2000, they paid public tribute to Wally Amos as having been an inspiration. On the twenty-fifth anniversary of Famous Amos, both Ben and Jerry traveled to New York's Central Park Zoo for an event executed by Rosica Strategic Public relations, where they thanked Amos for inspiring them, not only to get involved in causes, but also as a solid role model with a great brand persona and an authentic story.

"In the beginning, I wasn't really influenced by anyone, because I didn't know anything about business before we got into business," Jerry explained. "We didn't have any business education, so when we started, we were just feeling our way through it."

Jerry goes on to credit his partner. "Ben is so innovative and creative. He is not so constrained by conventional business thinking, or any *other* kind of conventional thinking. A lot of times, business people will tell you what they've done before, but they can't tell you about things that *haven't* been done before. Ben's attitude is that just because something hasn't been done this way before, it doesn't mean we shouldn't try it, or that it's not possible."

For his part, Ben Cohen explained that Martin Luther King, Jr. had been *his* inspiration. "He stood up and used his voice for social justice. Toward the end of his days he started preaching about what he called the 'Giant Triplets' of racism, militarism, and materialism. He felt that these were the things that we had to focus on countering. He started talking about militarization and the Pentagon budget as what he called 'the demonic sucking tube' that takes resources away from things that would truly benefit our society, such as spending money on education, welfare and housing."

Like Ben Cohen, Gary Hirshberg tends to draw his inspiration from outside the traditional business-school model.

> "People tend to think that you have to be smart, you have to be fast, you have to be a good marketer or good with numbers. I think you can hire all of that. I think what you really have to be is super-persistent."
>
> —Gary Hirshberg

"Even though I've built a $300-million-plus company, my mental orientation is still that I'm not really a business person," Hirshberg says. "I've always been, and thought of myself as, an activist, and I think the way I do business is the way that I express my activism."

Hirshberg went on to tell us, "For me, the inspiration that comes to the top of my mind every time someone asks is Nelson Mandela. In his book *Long Walk to Freedom*, he talks about having endured 26 years of unfair imprisonment, and having come out more peaceful, more committed, more dedicated, more powerful than ever before. The fact that he even *got out* with his spirit intact, having been in solitary through half that time, cut off from family, from children, from his wife, is amazing to me. With no real connection to the world that you and I take for granted every day, he came out a greater humanitarian than when he went in."

He described what he sees as the essential lesson that can be drawn from Mandela's terrible experience: "Mandela's ordeal teaches me a lesson of business that I've never taken for granted. This is persistence. It is probably the most underrated, but essential, virtue. People tend to think that you have to be smart, you have to be fast, you have to be a good marketer or good with numbers. I think you can hire all of that. I think what you really have to be is super-persistent."

Gary Hirshberg went on to tell us that the one business person whom he really admires is Yvon Chouinard, who founded the Patagonia outdoor clothing and gear company in 1972. The son of a French-Canadian blacksmith, Chouinard grew up in southern California, a dedicated outdoorsman and climber. He used his blacksmithing background to design and manufacture improved steel climbing pitons for use in the challenging cliffs of Yosemite National Park. He later established Patagonia, which offers a full line of outdoor products. A supporter of environmental causes, Chouinard turned Patagonia into the model of a socially responsible company.

"He is somebody with desire or intentions to be 'in business,' who built a business while sticking to his core values all the way through," Gary Hirshberg says. "From what I can tell, he is pretty much an unchanged person as a result of the whole exercise."

"My mom for sure, my dad from a creative standpoint, and from a confidence perspective," Bobbi Brown said, crediting both her parents. "My parents always taught me that I could do anything, even though they never expected me to overachieve. They taught me that I *could*, and they've always been there to support me. My parents and my grandparents have been incredible influences as far as being a good person and doing the right thing. My grandfather started out as a car salesman, and he later owned car dealerships in Chicago. He was constantly working. When he was not working, he was home sending out flyers and calling his customers, and I guess as a kid I watched that and that really was a part of it. My husband is also a huge influence in my personal life."

Outside of her family, Bobbi acknowledges Oprah Winfrey as an important influence. "She has been a very big inspiration in my personal life. I've been on her show. I've known her since she had a local show in Chicago. Every time I'm around her or see her, like everyone else in America, I say 'Wow, look at the positive things that you can do with power, influence, and success.'"

Jeff Taylor cited the influence of two of the most successful entrepreneurs in recent memory: Microsoft co-founder Bill Gates, and Virgin Atlantic founder Richard Branson. As with Oprah Winfrey, their names have become household words that are synonymous with both their own brands and with outstanding entrepreneurial success.

"I've watched Gates over the years, and he seems to have overcome image adversity, and has handled himself fairly gracefully," Taylor said, assessing Microsoft. "I like Richard Branson because he is an enthusiast as well as an entrepreneur. His enthusiasm is apparent through his work in many different dimensions. The way he promotes things that are 'bigger than big' is reflective of what I see in a powerful visionary as not only having the vision, but also the power to apply it. Branson has been able to do that. He really personifies the brand. The brand is him."

Indeed, Branson, who is both a student and a teacher of marketing, had outstanding instincts for public relations.

David Oreck, meanwhile, cites a business leader from an earlier generation. David Sarnoff joined the Marconi Wireless Telegraph Company of America as an office boy in 1906, and when it became the Radio Corporation of America (RCA) in 1919, he rose through the ranks to become its president in 1930. Known as the "General" for his management style, Sarnoff remained with the company until his retirement in 1970, building RCA into one of the largest companies in the world and a global leader in radio, television, and electronics.

"Sarnoff was my mentor and principle influence," Oreck explained, telling us of his own career with RCA in the 1950s. "He was a genius. He reminded me very much of the statement by Winston Churchill that you should never, never, never give up. He was a very hard worker, a strictly no-BS guy. If he ever caught you saying something or *not* saying something that you should, then you were history."

When we asked Wally Amos from whom he got inspiration, he said, "I've met so many people during my time, in many different industries. I've learned something, and have taken something away, from all of them. There are lessons to be learned from everyone you meet. Some become very memorable, and some don't, but they all become a part of your experience, and they're all incorporated into your life. They all become a part of the way you respond to life and a part of the way that you do business."

Amos named Harvey Mackay, the founder and chairman of Mackay Envelope Company, who is also a *New York Times* best-selling author, an acclaimed public speaker, and a columnist nationally syndicated with United Features. In 1959, Mackay purchased an insolvent envelope company with a dozen employees, three outdated folding machines, and a single printing press. Today, Mackay Envelope produces over four billion envelopes a year in three modern plants. Harvey Mackay himself has authored books such as *Swim with the Sharks Without Being Eaten Alive* and *Beware the Naked Man Who Offers You His Shirt.* According to *The New York Times*, these books are among the 15 top inspirational business books ever.

"He has set a really fine example," Amos said of Mackay. "He has tons of energy, and just goes a thousand miles a minute. Actually, I can't keep up with him. He's a great inspiration."

When we asked about influences in his personal life, Wally really opened up with some great stories.

"They're not necessarily famous, or people whom anybody would know," he said, getting into those who have inspired him personally. "There's a young man in Atlanta, Georgia, named Kerry Norwood who had sickle cell anemia. We met when he was about 11 years old. They had told him he would not live to be 13. Kerry Norwood is now 37, with two children. He's a great father and a fantastic person. He's in and out of the hospital, but his attitude is just so *strong*. He just keeps on going. He knows his body better than anybody I've ever met. Because he's so conscious of what he can and cannot do, he really takes care of his body. Kerry Norwood is constantly on my mind. We stay in touch, and I love him and respect him a lot."

Wally also mentioned a well-known artist he knows in Hawaii named Peggy Chun.

"Peggy's had ALS for several years, and she's at a point where she can't move any part of her body except her eyes," he says. "Yet,

> "We did not have a very good record of hiring people. We ended up with a few great people, but I have always said that our hiring percentage was about 50-50. We would have done just as well if we threw all of the applications up in the air and just picked that way."
>
> —Ben Cohen

she can communicate and she's so joyful. They've created a really intricate system for her to communicate. She has a computer that she can control by just concentrating on it with her eyes. When she lost control of her right hand, she learned how to paint with her left. When her left hand gave out, she had a pallet made for her mouth. She painted with the pallet in her mouth, and when she couldn't move her head anymore, she had people grab pieces of her hair and move her head in the direction that she told them to. Christine, my wife, goes over to be with Peggy once a week. She needs someone 24 hours a day, and there are 46 people who have volunteered to help her around the clock. They call them Peg's Legs."

In telling her story, Wally conveyed the lesson he had learned from Peggy. "I visited her one day when she could still speak," he told us. "She told me, 'Wally, I'm living with ALS, I'm not *dying* from it.' She's been a tremendous inspiration. There are a lot of those kinds of people whom I have met during my life who inspired me, and who made it impossible for me to pity myself, or to be anything but be positive."

Finding and Retaining Talented People

An important component of leadership comes in a leader's choice of a staff, especially senior management, to support the activities of the company, and in turn, the vision of the founder. In the early days of many companies, there is a point where it becomes evident that employees are essential. As Jerry Greenfield said, there was a point where he and Ben Cohen "realized that it wasn't possible for us to do everything ourselves."

As it is for many entrepreneurs, it was not easy to begin sharing the operations of the company with people who were not necessarily as passionate or committed as Ben and Jerry were.

"I had incredibly high standards for myself and at the beginning," Jerry reflects. "I was expecting everyone to hit those same standards, and then I realized that most people are not willing to sacrifice their entire lives for the business. I needed to start accepting less than what I regarded as 100 percent."

When we asked Ben and Jerry how they had found the great people with whom they surrounded themselves, Ben Cohen had a one word answer: "Luck."

"We did not have a very good record of hiring people," Ben told us. "We ended up with a few great people, but I have always said that our hiring percentage was about 50-50. We would have done just as well if we threw all of the applications up in the air and just picked that way."

Having established that Ben and Jerry actually did not throw the applications in the air, we went on to ask what criteria they really did use in the early days of hiring managers. We asked whether they based their decisions on the personalities of the applicants or on prior experience.

"We did it in different ways," Jerry told us. "We had an unusual mission for a company in that we needed people who were not only good with the business stuff, but who were also *equally* passionate about social values. This was a very unusual thing to look for when hiring, and it was very hard. We hired people with the business expertise, hoping to teach them the values and social mission of the company. We found it difficult if they didn't *already* have those kinds of values as a part of who they were as a person."

Despite their initial difficulty in developing hiring practices, Ben and Jerry said that having a casual work atmosphere helped them obtain the results they wanted.

"At the beginning we picked causes that Jerry and I were generally concerned about," Ben said of the values the company supported. "We had a mission statement that talked about a social mission, so this gave people an idea of what sorts of things would fit into that mission. In the beginning, we picked the causes that we were passionate about *personally*, and later on we got our input from people within the company. There came a time when we realized that we weren't going to be successful campaigning on these issues unless everyone in the company was brought into it. The best way to get them brought into it would be to get ideas from them."

For Wally Amos, as with the other entrepreneurs with whom we talked, hiring is intuitive, and not solely a matter of what is written on a resumé. "For me, it's how I feel about someone," he said. "It's a gut feeling and what I get from someone's spirit and/or energy."

He said that this had worked well for him through the years, but there had been some mistakes along the way.

"I had a guy who was working with me who I thought was the cat's meow," Amos laughed. "I did everything I could to support him and gave him great autonomy. The thing I learned from that is it's okay to trust people, but you have to watch them. You can't give people unlimited authority without checking up on them now and then. There have to be checks and balances, and if you can't do that, then you have to have someone who can."

Turning to a characterization of what he looks for in people he likes to hire, he continued: "I believe in hiring really skilled, quality people who have a good attitude. I also believe in hiring motivators who want to *do* things. You give them some parameters and then let them do it. I'm successful because of the people whom I hire and who work with me. I'm very limited in my skills, and I need a lot of people to help me be successful, to help with the other things that a business requires."

David Oreck answered our question about how he picked his staff by recalling when he had asked the same thing of David Sarnoff at RCA.

"How do you really know a guy when he comes in with an excellent resumé?" Oreck asked Sarnoff.

"You don't," Sarnoff replied. "You don't know him until you hire him, and you don't *really* know him until he disagrees with you."

"Assuming you used due diligence in hiring him, and assuming that you've checked out his references, and that you were satisfied with his abilities, I think it probably takes about a year to *really* know him," Oreck replied, when we asked him how long it actually takes to be sure whether someone is right for the job. "As far as the resumé goes, I've never had anybody put down someone as a reference who didn't like him. If a guy comes from a company whose profits increased $10 million in the five years he worked there, in all likelihood, it's a coincidence. He just happened to be around. It's conceivable that it did have something to do with him, but I always take that with a grain of salt."

Many managers and business leaders subscribe to the notion that the magic number is six months for a person's true potential to become evident. It typically does not happen overnight with relatively inexperienced people, but more seasoned staff and supervisors should demonstrate their potential qualities and skills from the get-go.

Gary Hirshberg is also skeptical of hiring someone solely on the basis of what he or she might say in a resumé. He too, prefers to go on the basis of instinct, his gut feeling.

"I don't believe you can hire anyone based on results because it's so easy to fake a resumé," Hirshberg told us emphatically. "Have you ever heard a bad reference for someone? It's a joke, that whole process. The fact that the references were offered by the candidate makes them right away less credible. You look at the individuals, you ask them some questions, and you look them in the eye. You scrutinize some of their references, of course, and you ask penetrating questions. I spend my time feeling them out, and also I try to find people on my own who really *do* know them. For example, I can often find a soccer coach in someone's community, and learn things that way if I need to. I coach three soccer teams. The soccer mafia is a pretty powerful way to connect."

Hirshberg added happily that executive hiring is a task that he doesn't often have to do.

"One of my sources of pride, and more materially, of success, has been that I don't have a lot of turnover at the senior level," he smiled. "My average vice president has been here seven to nine years, so I don't get to do this too often!"

"In some respect, we're two different companies here," Gary Hirshberg said of the Stonyfield Farm organization. "There's the manufacturing, processing, logistics and distribution side, or what I call the operations part of our business. Then there is the marketing and finance side, the more executive function. I don't tend to drill too deeply unless there is a problem such as consumer complaints or distribution issues. I don't tend to have a lot to say about whom the vice presidents hire, except in the areas of public relations and marketing, because these are really my forté. Here I'm very involved. Whenever a vice president wants me to meet somebody, I'm always available for interviews. When there is a key position such as a senior human-resources position or a senior plant engineer position, I will try to at least say hello. But it isn't so much to weigh in on the decision as much as it is to do a gut check."

In addition to their "gut check," many entrepreneurs and Fortune 500 companies swear by personality-profile services such as Persogenics or interview systems such as Topgrading. Persogenics is a system that quantifies the way people communicate and relate with each other for the purpose of increasing understanding. The roots of the Persogenics system lie in the research work begun by Dr. Ford A. Cheney and his associates in the late 1960s. They based their research on the pioneering efforts of such important figures in psychology as Dr. Hermann Rorschach and Dr. Gordon W. Allport. However, they took the research one step further by profiling not just the primary style, but also the secondary, and their initial efforts paid off with a higher profiling accuracy than other personality profilers had achieved. Dr. Cheney and his research team of physicians and PhDs at Keystone Research Labs went on to develop a job profile, while applying their expertise to discover new ways to apply Persogenics. The Persogenics Job Profile is a tool that enables managers and supervisors to identify the requirements a job will make of whomever is chosen for the position, fully defining the amount of time that will be demanded of the individual in areas such as attention to detail, interaction with people, tasks requiring creativity, and every other facet of the nature of work.

Topgrading, meanwhile, is described as "a means of packing entire companies with high performers, from senior management to minimum-wage employees." As Brad Smart points out, "Topgrading training and topgrading interviews result in up to 90 percent success in hiring high performers, 'A-players.' After decades of fine-tuning topgrading tools, processes, and topgrading training, there is no doubt that shareholders of all companies benefit from topgrading. And, our topgrading coaching methodology gives all managers the best chance of becoming, or remaining, high performers themselves."

Geoff Smart, Brad's son, is chairman and CEO of his own topgrading company, completely independent of his father. He too is an excellent source on the art and science of hiring. A management assessment, coaching, and executive learning firm, ghSMART has offices across North America and clients that include leading private-equity investors, hedge-fund managers, Fortune 500 CEOs, and billionaire entrepreneurs. According to Brad, ghSMART is "The best management-assessment firm in the world."

We asked Jeff Taylor how he selected the top people at Monster, acknowledging that many of the people who have worked with him have been phenomenal.

"I met someone on a T-ball field, I met someone on a plane, and I found some people on Monster," he smiled. "I've met a number of people through referrals. I'm not picky about where I meet great people, and I'm constantly thinking about recruiting in every environment that I'm in."

When we asked him whether he personally chose top executives—or whether he delegated that job to someone else within the organization whose primary focus was on the hiring process—he told us that this had transitioned over time, but that he still likes to stay close to the process.

"Initially, everyone was personally selected," he said. "As time has gone by, people who I have working for me, or in some cases working beside me, have made these selections. The process is at its strongest when you're as close as possible to the point of interaction with new employees. You never get to know employees well if you don't get to interview them, and to have that respect and rapport-building before they work side by side with you."

As for the criteria he uses when selecting personnel, we asked whether he focuses more on personality or achievements and results, he told us that it was a combination of the two.

"I tend to explore some aspects of a resumé, or some aspect of a person's personality," Taylor explained. "Based on the way they handle that aspect, I can learn a lot about how they would handle something else in their lives. For example, if a person is a marathon runner, then what I look for is whether the person might be an interesting candidate because of his or her interests. Would the person be an interesting candidate if he or she is a runner? Does that transfer over into other stuff in his or her life?"

This parallels some of the highly effective methods that are utilized by Geoff Smart and his firm.

Like Jeff Taylor, Jerry Baldwin looks at executive hiring as more a matter of resource management than simply picking an employee. "Hiring professionals is often a question of convincing them to work for you," Baldwin said. "Today, with Peet's Coffee, we are a fairly small company with big aspirations. We're always looking for people who have succeeded at a much higher level so they can help take us to that new level."

As with many entrepreneurs, Baldwin spent a good deal of time in formulating ways of finding people who had the right skill set, and who were also receptive to the philosophy of the company. He recalls a time when Starbucks was hiring for the job of comptroller, a position that would later become vice president of finance.

"I had headhunters track down six people, I interviewed them all, reduced it to three, and offered the job to one guy," Baldwin told us. "He then told Gordon Bowker and me that he had decided he was just too risk-averse for the job, and he backed out. I concentrated on the other two guys and picked one based on how he analyzed things. I recall a crucial moment when I asked him what he would do in a specific situation. His response was 'I don't know the business, but this is how I would go find the answer,' instead of saying, 'Oh yeah, this is what I'd do.' And he gave us five years of very good work."

Baldwin went on to cite three men who have influenced the way that he looks at human resources issues: Rene McPherson, Douglas McGregor and Eric Berne. McPherson was an executive with the Dana Corporation, an auto-parts manufacturer. In the late 1960s, he converted Dana into a model of productivity. In a famous move, he burned a foot-high stack of operating manuals, replacing it with a single-page sheet of "Forty Thoughts" covering behavior and attitude. He prompted employees to initiate their own production goals and set up an employee stock program. During his dozen years in the chairmanship, Dana's revenues increased five-fold. He later served as Dean of the Stanford University Graduate School of Business.

"Rene McPherson was one of the first people who started to think about employees as a resource," Baldwin explained. "Before that, there was no engagement on the part of most companies with their employees. You came, you worked, you got paid, you got a pension, you retired, you got a gold watch. There wasn't this sense of belonging that a lot of us look for today. In my hierarchy of values, getting people engaged and learning about the business is important. I don't have a business education, so most of what I've learned came by way of reading, or by taking a lot of short classes."

We could not agree more with Baldwin's notion that "getting people engaged and learning about the business is important." In our business, we know that learning results in employees who are both happy and engaged. Groups such as the Entrepreneurs' Organization, the Young Presidents' Organization, Vistage (formerly The Executive Committee), the Women Presidents' Organization, and others provide ample educational opportunities and offer support based on the experiences of other business leaders.

Douglas McGregor, the second person whom Baldwin cites, was a social psychologist and management professor at the Massachusetts Institute of Technology's Sloan School of Management. His 1960 book, *The Human Side of Enterprise,* significantly motivated management habits. McGregor developed the dual and opposing concepts of workplace behavior that he called "Theory X" and "Theory Y." McGregor believed that under Theory X, employees lack initiative and require supervision. They are motivated by the threat of losing their job and by financial incentives. Conversely, under Theory Y, people are inherently self-motivated, usually creative, and often resourceful if given a chance. Baldwin clearly believes in Theory Y.

Eric Berne was a Canadian-born psychiatrist who is best known for developing Transactional Analysis (TA), a way of looking at interpersonal relationships that categorizes them into three "ego-states," which Berne called Parent, Adult, and Child. In looking at these relationships, Berne saw recurring patterns which he called "games." His theories and conclusions were summarized in his 1964 best-selling book, *Games People Play*. He went on to form the International Transactional Analysis Association.

"Each of these ways of communicating had characteristics that in a way predicted outcomes," Baldwin said, referring to Berne's three ego-states. "The child, of course, is not mature and is often rebellious—asking 'Why can't I do it this way?' The parent is judgmental and controlling. When hiring people and turning them into managers, you often find that the only pattern that they have had for being a manager is their parents' activity. What Berne theorized is that you learned how to be a parent and how to be a child by the time you were six years old because you've established patterns of communication with your own parents. If you look at kids before they start to speak, they're really taking it in. You look at one- or two-year-old kids, and they're thinking and reacting. Kids learn how to push their parents' buttons, and of course, the parents always fall for it. We want to move away from either of those styles of communications and speak adult-to-adult or peer-to-peer. I couldn't count the number of hours and dollars that went into training people to speak in this way with other people. It worked *up*, as well as it worked *down*. If you always had an equal-to-equal form of communication, it would really be effective. What that built, what that engendered, was a feeling of equality, dignity, and value on the part of everybody who worked there."

When we asked Andy Spade how he and Kate attract the best people to their staff, he said that the first thing that came to mind was the work environment.

"Having a great environment where there are bright and challenging people," was Spade's answer. "I think challenging them intellectually and challenging them creatively are important. We're a young company, so we have a lot of opportunity. I think this attracts talented people because they can make an impact on the business. In a bigger company, you can't have as much impact. Someone once said to me, 'Go where you're needed most.' A lot of times when I talk to people, I tell them that this is a place where you are needed. You can really have an impact, and you can see real tangible differences in the business after being part of it for a year or two. I've always felt good when I have an impact on something, and I think everyone feels better when they can see results from what they've done."

Spade went on to say that he felt that it was important for people to be acknowledged for their contribution to the organization. When asked how this was done within the business that he and Kate have built, he explained: "We have a process here which merits people not only for how they perform, but also for their problem-solving ability, and their willingness to take risks. Another part of the process is thanking them, and being a part of their life—being someone they can relate to and talk to about things."

He went on to say that, for many years, he and Kate were directly involved in hiring all of the company's employees, but that eventually they delegated the hiring of all but the upper and mid-level managers. "In the beginning, everybody was doing everything, but when the business got to a certain size, we thought it was necessary to put in levels of management," he said.

"Kate or I may meet some of the more junior-level people, depending on the department in which they're working," he said. "Kate talks to everyone in design, and I talk to everybody in the creative department. I do believe in meeting everybody. I think that this is an owner's job. The most important thing in a company is hiring the right people because that's what makes you better. The only asset we have is people and that's *all* we have."

When we asked about hiring criteria, Andy quickly told me that he and Kate hire only "*nice*, talented people."

"If you're nice but you're not talented, you can't work here," he said simply. "To say that you can work here only if you're talented and nice is not a fresh approach. It's understood. You have to go beyond that. You have to hire on values, and know who the person is. You can teach someone a skill. They often come from another industry, and we can teach them a skill, but you can't teach them values, and you can't teach them how to be a certain way. You can't teach them how to be honest."

We asked him how he does it, and he told us that he evaluates people on their personalities and any other values. He also said that he tries to see himself in the place of the applicants.

"Sometimes you see a diamond in the rough who just hasn't been given the opportunity," he said. "Maybe they've been in the wrong position. We hit our stride when we came here. We were doing well before, but we never took off like this until we found a good place for *us* to fit. There are people out there who are probably hitting their heads against the walls because they're in the wrong place at the wrong time. They have huge talent and you put them in another role and they shine."

When we asked Bobbi Brown whether she was still involved in the hiring process, she said that, like Andy and Kate Spade, she definitely made the decisions in upper-level management. When I asked her about her hiring criteria, she said that personality is extremely important.

"I think personality is as important, if not *more* important, as keeping your head down and focusing on the job," Bobbi told us. "There are a lot of people who can get the job done, but we're a team, a huge team. Whether it's organizing the manicures for the week, or getting a new product out, or coming up with new ideas, or trying to fix something that's a mess, it's all teamwork. I've had this argument with people who are not in my business, and who are straight 'marketers,' or product-development people. In this business, if you don't understand the beauty or fashion business, you're not going to get it. So, personality is *really* important."

Bobbi gave us the example of Maureen Case, who was hired in 2002 as president of Bobbi Brown Worldwide.

"When I first met her, she walked in my door and we were finishing each other's sentences. I had a president at the time, but I told Maureen she should come in and be my head of marketing. She said she'd love to. When she became my head of marketing, I knew she would be the right president. Estée Lauder, our parent company, did not have the confidence in her that I did, so she was acting president for a year. She doubled our business. It's a case of someone whom you really enjoy, and whose opinion you trust, and with whom you have a creative collaboration."

As with Kate Spade, Bobbi Brown and others, Jim Koch

believes that it is important for employees to be an integral part of the company culturally. "Every month we have a week-long orientation for people who have just joined the company," he told us. "If you join Boston Beer Company, I want your first experience to be two hours with the founder, telling you about the culture and values of this company that you just joined. On the first morning of the orientation, I spend two hours with all the new people. I go through the culture, which includes mission statement, values, and vision. Everybody remembers their first day on a new job. I want to use that opportunity to be explicit about who we are and what our values and culture are. At the end of the day at 5:00 p.m., I'll spend two more hours with them, and we'll do a beer-tasting. We'll talk about different styles of beer and how to taste beer. We'll taste all of the different styles of beer that we make. I'll explain to them how they are made, what the ingredients are, and I'll give them some terminology around it."

Having exposed people to the culture and the products, Koch gets the newly hired personnel involved in actually making the product. "I'm such a big proponent of trying to expose people to the culture that our orientation includes two days of brewing beer. Everybody goes to the brewery and spends two days. Whether you're in accounting, sales, logistics, or whatever, you learn how to make beer. You have to learn what goes into our beers, and *why* they taste the way they do. This is my way of telling them that, even though we have all these words on a piece of paper, they are important enough to me that I'm going to take time every month to go through them with everybody. I want your first experience at Boston Beer Company to be our exploring those cultures and values together."

When I asked what he looks for in a potential employee, Jim

Koch explained that Boston Beer Company tries to hire people based on who they are.

"You need a minimum level of skill," he says. "But people don't succeed or fail because of their skill level. They succeed or fail because of their behavioral traits. A person might have a very impressive resumé, but he or she may not have self-awareness and ability to discern his or her effect on others. It's not a cookie cutter, though, because we've had quite different people who were successful in different ways."

On the important issue of delegating to his staff, Jim Koch told us: "I usually consult with the team, but there are things that go to the culture, the values, and the quality of the beer. These are the things that I worry about—the culture of the company and the quality of the beer. These decisions at the end of the day have to be mine."

"We have a great process for finding people," David Neeleman said when we asked how involved he is in hiring management for JetBlue. "We really try to hire *attitude*, so we use what we call 'Targeted Selection.' The hardest things to do are to change someone's behavior and attitude. There has been a lot of programming that has gone into that person in terms of genetics or whatever, so we to try hire a good attitude. It's more attitude than personality. Personality sounds too superficial. It's really attitude. Is the person a positive person? Is he or she someone who looks at the glass half-full instead of half-empty?"

When asked to elaborate, Neeleman told us that JetBlue likes to hire the "can-do" person.

"We hire someone who will cross over areas of responsibility to get things done," he explained. "If we get in a crisis mode at the airport during a big storm or a blackout, and we need more people, we'll send out an SOS and get 50 to 60 off-duty people out to the airport to help out fellow crew members. These are people who will drop everything to go help. They're not people who will just shrug 'I got my duty, I'm done, I'm moving on.'"

Many of the entrepreneurs with whom we spoke acknowledged that they strive for an interactive and collaborative atmosphere. Continuing this line of thought by looking into the concerns that result from this sort of environment, we asked how people approached the issue of conflict within their companies.

Managing Conflict

David Neeleman told us that within JetBlue this situation is referred to as "pushback."

"I wouldn't say 'conflict is conflict'," Neeleman explained. "I would say 'open dialogue where you can really speak up, speak your mind, and you can do this without any kind of retribution.' Of course, you better be prepared and you better know what you're talking about. If you continually bring stuff up, and you don't know what you're talking about, then that's not going to help your cause. When you do this, you're not going to have the kind of respect that is required to be an officer in this company."

"I think it's healthy, but it's hard to do," Ben Cohen acknowledged. "Some people are better at managing conflict than others. It's very helpful for an organization and for families. People have to learn how to have conflict. Some conflict is good, but it can also be bad."

Bobbi Brown believes that contrasting views and candor are highly productive. "I love it," she told us. "I love people who say what's on their mind."

David Oreck agrees, telling us, "A difference of opinion is healthy. I've encouraged people to give their views. However, once the top person has made the decision, that's just the way it is. Once that's been made, I expect everybody to fall into line for the common good, irrespective of whether the decision aligns with his or her original position or not. Hopefully, the guy who makes the decisions is right more often than not."

Like Oreck, Gary Hirshberg believes that differences of opinion have their place, but that such disagreements should be finite. He told us: "It's good to have people disagreeing to a point, but it's also good to have resolution. I'm not a big meeting guy, and I'm not into 'process.' This is probably a weakness, but I think it's common among entrepreneurs. Air your views, gather the data needed, and try to make your case. But then let's just make a decision and move on. I think prolonging conflict or dispute makes the conflict counterproductive."

In Jon Krakauer's book, *Into Thin Air: A Personal Account of the Mt. Everest Disaster,* he points out the inherent danger of creating a culture where people don't question the status quo, or don't feel the freedom to discuss options. While Krakauer's is a dramatic illustration, the business implications are obvious and relevant for managers and business owners alike.

Accountability, Measuring Results, and Goal Setting

Holding people accountable after they are hired is an important, yet often overlooked, aspect of human-resource management. Accountability can be described as essential to the success of any business organization.

Gary Hirshberg told us that the performance of those he does hire is measured in executive team meetings that are held twice a month, and in monthly reviews of financial and quality results. There is also an "Ops Team," comprising four vice presidents directly involved in operations, who meet weekly. "I'm not in the meeting every week," Hirshberg said. "But I pop in and out of it as my schedule allows."

His company also uses weekly flash reports. Put out by the accounting department, these contain data on factors ranging from recent performance to current distribution. The vice presidents in each area have other types of reports depending on the disciplines.

Jack Stack, the founder and CEO of SRC Holdings and the author of *The Great Game of Business* and *A Stake in the Outcome: Building a Culture of Ownership for the Long-Term Success of Your Business*, told us that he openly shares his numbers with all employees. His targets are also discussed openly, and these are the benchmarks toward which everyone works. He invites CEOs from all over the globe to see firsthand how this works and why.

Stack believes that four of the most hated words to every supervisor, manager, and owner in business today are "It's not my job!" He goes on to note that these "words do more damage to the productivity of your business than ever."

He also believes that organizations separate themselves from others in their industry and affect change before change is required by removing these four words from the employee's language, and by building a true culture of ownership. He describes this as "a culture where employees feel like it is their company, where the job they do every day has a direct impact on the financial performance of the organization—and, in turn, on their standard of living."

When we asked Wally Amos to elaborate on how he holds people accountable for executing and reaching goals, he told us, "You have criteria that you want to establish—not only the criteria but the way you have to *meet* those criteria. You have to set boundaries that everyone can buy into. How can you hold someone accountable for something that he or she is not buying into? You set those boundaries and criteria and each person establishes goals that we feel are reachable and that becomes a benchmark in the way you treat people, customers, and employees. You have to create procedures by which you can make corrections to achieve your goals in running your business in a way that is more profitable, and more beneficial to everyone."

> "You develop goals or criteria that would specifically fit the type of a job. It is absolutely vital to set goals."
>
> **—David Oreck**

Discussing the notion of measuring for accountability, David Oreck told us that his company measures different things in different job categories.

"You hold salesmen accountable for sales," he says. "In the accounting department or the credit department, performance has to do with collections or accounts receivable. You develop goals or criteria that would specifically fit the type of a job. It is absolutely vital to set goals. Every business is always trying to grow to be more profitable, so, you look for things that are important, such as ways to expand your distribution in a given area, for example."

We asked Bobbi Brown what sort of benchmarks or goals she sets for evaluating performance, and what she looks for in yearly reviews. "For me, it's just that someone is *there*," she says, "someone who is completely on the ball. Of course, sales people are totally account-able. It really depends on who happens to be right for the job."

When Jerry Baldwin looks at how he holds his personnel accountable, he applies many of the human-resources ideas that he learned from Rene McPherson, Douglas McGregor, and Eric Berne. "The idea is to communicate regularly," he says. "We had instituted a system of performance review, the aspects of which were that the individual reviewed himself or herself, and you reviewed him or her as well. Then you sat down and you talked about it. The other aspect is that humans are really good at picking out what's wrong, and I don't know why that is. I'm good at it too. We limited the number of things that they could write down on the piece of paper so that there were only as many bad things as there were good. This way, we ended up talking about big issues instead of minutiae. Based on the idea that everybody wants to do a good job, this frequent com-munication in a way helped people evaluate themselves. The ideal situation is to have people realize they're not getting the job done, and they leave rather than your having to sack them."

He went on to say that how often people are reviewed is depen-dent on their level of responsibility, but that he is a believer in frequent reviews. "The lower the level, the more frequent the review should be, because you're typically dealing with less experience. I wonder whether you can over communicate with people. I suppose you could spend too much time talking, but if you talked to some-body for a half-hour four times a year, would that be too much? Of course not. However, realistically it doesn't get done because it's such a project to review all your people."

In our interactions with highly successful companies—large and small—regular reviews and communications are a common trait.

David Neeleman told us that he categorizes accountability as critically important. "It's really the essence of business as it really is—effective leadership," he explained.

To illustrate his philosophy on this question, and a chief executive's role in addressing it, he went on to relate his pre-JetBlue experience, when he was working in operations at Southwest Airlines.

"I tried to do everything," he recalls. "If a plane was broken somewhere, I was calling Boeing, trying to find the part. I ran back and forth, and I really just burned myself out. I became overwhelmed because I didn't have the kind of quality people whom I should have had in the different positions. One day when they were canceling flights because of ice storms in St. Louis, I was on the dispatch watching all of this go on. I asked myself, 'Wow, I wonder if Herb Kelleher knows all this stuff is going on. He should be down here.'"

"Then I realized," Neeleman continued, "there's nothing Herb can do down here. He needs to be up there looking at the vision of the company and thinking about that. This is when I learned a great lesson about delegating authority to deal with problems such as those that I was observing that day in St. Louis. Herb had people who reported to him, who gave him an accounting of the on-time percentage on a weekly or monthly basis, and they were held accountable for this. If it slips, they'd have to explain. If they didn't have good explanations, he'd find someone else to do that job. But when you delegate, you have to hold people accountable, and *you* have to set the standard. They have to know what the standard is, and meet that standard. If they don't meet it, there needs to be a reason why, and it is up to you to figure out the solution."

In this, we are reminded of the words of Michael Gerber, the entrepreneur and author of *The E-Myth Revisited: Why Most Small Businesses Don't Work and What to Do About It*. His "E-Myth" concept suggests that a business should be "a vehicle to bring its owner more life, through the core principles of: Life, Objectivization, Working *On* the Business—Not *In* It, Systemization, and Business Development."

Gerber's E-Myth point of view embodies his commitment to personal growth and "the realization that a business owner's purpose in life can be actualized through his or her business."

We followed up by asking Neeleman what steps he has taken within his organization to ensure accountability. He explained that, within JetBlue, there is a division of labor at the highest level, wherein Neeleman himself handles the accounting side, which includes sales and marketing, as well as reservations. Meanwhile, his chief executive officer takes care of the day-to-day operations of the airline, including aircraft certification, airports, pilots, flight attendants, mechanics, and technicians.

"It's measurable," Neeleman said of the operations side of JetBlue's business. "We have on-time percentages, we have cancelled-flight percentages, we have delay percentages, and then we have customer surveys that come in."

He described how things work on the operations side, where meetings such as those that Verne Harnish describes as "daily huddles," take place. "Every day there is a 7:30 a.m. briefing with direct reports on the phone with the CEO for thirty minutes. Everyone accountable is on the line. They discuss progress, including what happened yesterday, and what's going to happen today. As far as my own management style with my own direct reports, they know that we have certain number targets, such as load-factor targets."

David Neeleman told me that JetBlue has adopted a five-part "Principles of Leadership" program, which is a customized learning and development program based on five key expectations of JetBlue leaders.

"Each leader, from the supervisor level up to the CEO, has to live these principles of leadership," he explained. "Every single person has these principles of leadership around his or her neck on his or her ID tag. These five principles are: Treat your people right, do the right thing, communicate with your team, encourage initiative and innovation, and inspire greatness in others. Each has a subset. For example, under 'treat your people right,' we work to create an environment where crew members feel that their efforts make a difference. We involve crew members in the plans and decisions that affect them, we encourage teamwork, and we encourage each leader to motivate the team he or she leads to choose a goal together, and to recognize and celebrate accomplishments. The leaders coach their crew members to continuously improve, and they spend time in the field, so they are there for their crew members."

Neeleman walks the walk and flies the skies himself to ensure the optimal customer experience. He flies often to see *and feel* how the airline is doing. The lesson in this, as Neeleman describes it, is that each of JetBlue's crew members has been given a tangible and well-defined set of principles that clearly define accountability.

"We give them access to all these principles of leadership," he told us. "If a specific leader is not doing these things, we can sit down with him and tell him, for example, that he hasn't been in the field for three weeks. Everybody knows what is expected of him or her. If someone says, 'I don't know what you're talking about,' I can respond that the five principles are right there on your ID badge, right around you're neck, and we can pull it out, and we can go over it."

David Neeleman's message to his management is simple: "I tell them to hold their leaders accountable because they're going to hold *you* accountable too. If you show up late to work and you're not doing things, then you're not going to be here either. It's all about accountability. We feel strongly about accountability." As business leaders, we realize that a large part of the challenge lies in keeping the plates spinning—so none falls and breaks.

"Some of that comes back to the culture," Jeff Taylor explained. "If someone really 'catches fire' to the culture, how you measure the productivity of that person is nearly irrelevant. If he or she is captured and on fire in the culture, then he or she is ready to go. You don't have to measure it at all—you have to figure out how to harness his or her energy!"

Too Many Meetings?

Another aspect of corporate culture that is common in organizations of the size that we are profiling in this book is staff meetings. For some, they are viewed as a necessary evil, while for others, they are an important part of communication. While all of the entrepreneurs with whom we spoke have used meetings routinely, their opinions vary on the value of meetings generally. For instance, when we asked David Neeleman whether typical companies have too few meetings or too many, he quickly responded that there were too many. Wally Amos used almost the same words when he told us "I think there are too many. I don't know if anything *ever* gets done!"

Jerry Greenfield told us: "I think we had a lot of meetings. We were very collaborative. Some people might say *too* collaborative. It was not always clear how decisions were made, or who made decisions. It was somewhat of a touchy-feely kind of thing."

Jeff Taylor said that he felt companies generally "have too many, and I think they are too long. I find that meetings are a good way to check progress, but inefficient when it comes to actually getting the job done. I much prefer groups rather than lectures or meetings. Groups have occasional meetings to check on the progress of the rest of the groups. I like an early-morning meeting to kickoff each day that is held basically to inspire people to go and get their jobs done for the day. I like an all-hands meeting. I think they work at the beginning of a start-up, as you are building out your business concepts. Later on, meetings can be about sales and revenues and profits—and ultimately can look at employee satisfaction, customer satisfaction and market penetration as ways to measure the success of the company."

Therefore, it is widely acknowledged that meetings need, as Harnish states, "a rhythm, purpose, and time limit to be effective and to improve productivity."

There are several resources to tap into, such as Gazelles.com, for tools that can improve meetings and how employees and management view them. One thing is clear: As our business leaders have concurred, there is just as much danger, if not more, in avoiding communications as in over-communicating.

Showing Vulnerability

An important question involved in dealing with employees is

whether the boss should show vulnerability with his people. Most of the entrepreneurs with whom we spoke were willing to do this, sharing the point of view of Jerry Baldwin, who told us simply: "I pretty much wear my feelings on my sleeve."

Like Baldwin, Gary Hirshberg told us that he is not reticent about showing his vulnerability. "I'm governed by this idea that you have to be human," he told us. "Most of the people at Stonyfield Farm are strangers to me now. It wasn't that way long ago when I knew everybody, and I knew their families. But at our rate of growth, I don't know more than half the people here anymore, and they don't know me. Therefore, I have to be, first and foremost, upbeat and positive. Secondly, I have to be tuned into their wave-lengths as they're looking at the minutiae and I'm looking at the big picture. But, I don't shy away from the expressive. I don't think anybody would ever accuse me of pulling any punches or hiding how I'm feeling."

On the other hand, Jim Koch told us that he would never display vulnerability on purpose. "My grandmother always said humility was a virtue," he recalls. "It's a tricky thing. One of the things I learned at Outward Bound is that the leader is never tired, the leader is never depressed, and the leader is never pessimistic. If you're going to be that way, go do it somewhere else, but don't do it in front of your people."

Koch perceives a danger in allowing your people to see you exposed. "You can be modest, but you just can't tell them that you're not sure we're going to make it," he said. "I learned that in Outward Bound: Whatever level of energy and optimism you have, the other people will have a lower level. You can't ask *them* to pick you up."

When we asked Jerry Greenfield whether he and Ben shared their vulnerability with the employees, and whether they were reticent to share financial concerns with their people, Jerry told us that he considered these as two different things.

"I think we showed people our vulnerabilities because we were a small business, and we were not really organized in a hierarchical way," he recalled. "It was a very casual, friendly, informal atmosphere and we were clearly regular guys. We didn't dress in suits and we were very approachable. On the other hand, if the company was on the edge of going out of business or something like that, we didn't want to scare people. If everyone needed to pitch in and help out, we would certainly share whatever conditions were creating that."

On the issue of sharing his vulnerability with his team, Jeff Taylor readily described himself as "an open book."

"I think people know my struggles, what makes me happy and what makes me sad," he says. "I spend a lot of time with my key people understanding their personal lives, understanding what makes them tick and what gets *them* excited. I move about within that. It's not uncommon for me to take the first 20 minutes of a meeting to talk about absolutely nothing, rather than getting right to the agenda. When I say 'absolutely nothing,' I mean what's going on in the world, how people's weekends went, or a person's individual challenge, and how we can help solve it."

Bobbi Brown told us that she considers showing her vulnerability to her executive team to be "probably my worst attribute." When we asked her to elaborate, she explained that she felt this way because of her inherent openness. "Everybody knows who my favorites are," she said. "Unfortunately, if I don't like something or

> "I decided years ago that I needed to be consistent with everyone. I need to show the same face and the same personality with everyone."
>
> —Wally Amos

someone, you know it."

She went on to say that she is also very open about admitting mistakes. "I'm very honest about that," she says. "If I hate something, and I signed off on it, I take total responsibility for it. I'm a real person even in my business, so I have my good days and my bad days."

Wally Amos told us that he is very open about showing his vulnerability with his employees and executive management team, but that he feels it is important to do so equally with everyone.

"This is who I am. I'm not going to pretend that I'm someone else," he says. "I decided years ago that I needed to be consistent with everyone. I need to show the same face and the same personality with everyone. I meet too many people to do otherwise."

David Neeleman told us that he tries to be frank with people, very up-front. "I've learned, from being at a public company, that you have to show restraint in what you say to people," he said. "But for the most part, when I speak to our crew members in our monthly 'pocket sessions,' I'm as honest as I can be, and direct about the challenges. At one pilot meeting involving maybe seventy pilots, I was particularly upset about some cancellations that we had to make. I was disturbed to the point where they thought I was mad at them, and that perception spread throughout the company. I had to send an email to all the pilots explaining that I was not mad at them, but mad at the fact that the weather was affecting us and that we weren't as structurally capable of handling it as maybe we should have been. I think that apologizing for a misunderstanding of this sort raises your ability to lead a couple of notches in the eyes of your team." As witnessed by the company's challenges in 2007, Neeleman was overly frank when disclosing too much information, which impacted the company's credibility. Perception *is* reality.

Family and Belief Systems

Nowhere is the phrase "lonely at the top" more applicable than among entrepreneurs. By definition, an entrepreneur is usually a loner, facing an often hostile competition, while backed by staff who are not his or her equals within the organizational structure. Against this backdrop, the entrepreneur needs the support of family and friends, even as the hours required by the business often preclude quality family time.

In the early days of any company, the founder is consumed, with all of his or her energies and time focused on building that business. When I asked Jerry Greenfield how many hours he was putting in during the time that he and Ben were building their business, he responded with "As many hours as there are in a day."

We asked our entrepreneurs whether or not they had any regrets, looking back on the time they were able to spend—or *not* able to spend—with friends and family during the growth period of their businesses. We were interested to learn that most did not.

Jerry Greenfield said, "No, I don't have any regrets. Both Ben and I spent a ton of time doing the business in the beginning, but I feel amazingly lucky to have had the opportunity that we have had. Ben and I worked really hard and we were both very dedicated to what we did."

Ben Cohen told us, "I think it was difficult for me to have balance in my life between working and family, but I don't really have regrets for the amount of time I put into the business. It's not a thought that comes into my head. I did spend enough time with family. There were years when I didn't spend enough time with my friends because I was busy. As I said, the thought didn't cross my mind that I was spending too much time doing this, or that it was unhealthy, or that I should have been doing something else. It never reached that point. In the years since, I have reconnected with my friends."

To the contrary, Jeff Taylor told us, "I do have some regrets about not spending enough time with family and friends. I'm divorced and probably at some level that is because of some choices that were made."

When he was asked whether he felt, in retrospect, that he had spent enough time with family and friends while he was building Starbucks and Peet's, Jerry Baldwin's answer was an emphatic "Of course not. I can't say that I was particularly well-balanced. I was absolutely focused too much on work." As to whether he feels balanced today, he gave an honest, and equally emphatic, "No." He then went on to explain, "For me to answer that question affirmatively would be too smug. It would be smug to say, 'My life is perfect, man, I got it wired. I give just the right amount of attention to my family.' No, I don't."

When we asked Gary Hirshberg whether he thought he spent enough time with his family and friends while he was building the business, his one-word answer was simply "Never."

He did go on to qualify this answer by saying, "On the other hand, I coach all three kids and that's given me some real quality time and a quality relationship. I know them intimately, and I also know all their friends. And I have really been in their lives in a way that other parents aren't."

David Oreck responded to the question of having spent enough time with friends and family by

> **The balancing of the business and family halves of one's life require a structure that is often elusive.**

telling us, "I'm better now than I ever was, but I simply think that, to be successful, especially when you start from scratch without financial backing to speak of, you *have to* really devote yourself to your business. If you do, you're not going to have the time, as much time, to spend with your family. I don't say that that's the right thing; it's just the way it is."

Oreck shared an illustrative anecdote: "I recall years ago there was a young guy who was the head of a magazine and who asked me, 'What does it take for me to be successful here?' I told him, 'Well, first you've got to get divorced.' I just wanted to shake him up with that one-liner, but I went on to tell him that, if you do all of the things that you *should do* to help ensure your business success, that time has got to come from somewhere. You've got to be thinking about it even when you're not on the job. I don't say that that's good, I'm just saying that, to me, it's just a fact."

"Fortunately, I've had a very good relationship with my three sons," Oreck explained. "I think occasionally one of them will say, 'You know, you didn't go to my soccer game like I thought you should have, and I felt pretty bad about that,' but I think as they got older they came to realize that I was doing my thing and it was in their interest for me to have done that. I think that I've become a little softer, and they've become more understanding. I'm glad that I've lived long enough to try to make up for the things that I didn't do when I was thirty."

The balancing of the business and family halves of one's life requires a structure that is often elusive. As David Neeleman says, "You have to have rules. If you don't have rules, then you get yourself into trouble. One rule I have is that I don't work weekends. The airline runs 24 hours a day, so I could easily get sucked into working weekends. If it's a crisis, I'll work weekends, but mainly this is something I leave to people who know what they're doing."

Neeleman explained that he doesn't travel as much as he once did. "I try to make it home and to spend time with the family," he said. "We have family scripture study and prayer time at about 7:30 or 8:00 each night. We take probably three full-week vacations a year, so we spend a lot of time together. I do value the time with my family."

With friends, it's another story. David Neeleman told us, "I don't really have any friends. I don't think you really can have a lot of friends and have a big family like I do, or have a business that's kind of consuming you on a day-to-day basis."

"We definitely try to spend a lot of time with our family and friends," Andy Spade said of himself and Kate. "Fortunately, some family work with us and friends are nearby, which helps. We actually work with a lot of friends too. A lot of them are here, but even outside we do spend a lot of time with them. We meet them after work. They come by the loft, we talk to them, and we go out. I don't think we sacrificed any big relationships. Friends are a big part of our business and life. I would say Kate spends more time with her family than I do with mine, because my family is all based on the West Coast. I wish I could spend more time with my family, but it's just a logistical thing."

"I could not work five days a week, and I could not be home five days a week, so I feel really lucky that I have a balance and flexibility," Bobbi Brown told us. "I do spend a lot of time with family and friends, and I do feel as though I spend enough. Sometimes, just after a ten-day vacation, it seems like *too much*. This week happens to be, personally, the slowest week of the year, so I had an extra day home. I cooked and I cleaned up the kids' toys. I'm dying to get back to work. There's nothing else to clean at my house."

When we asked Wally Amos whether he had any regrets about the time commitment he invested in his business, he responded by saying, "I don't have a regret mindset. I think that everything that I've done has gotten me to today, and today is the greatest day of my life because I'm here to experience today. I don't have regrets."

Amos said enthusiastically, "Everything has been a learning experience. I've helped a lot of people on my journey and have been helped by many people along the way. Carl Sandburg says that the past is but a bucket of ashes, and that's very true. The past is over, you can't change it. All that people do is talk about it a lot, but I'm too busy living in the present and enjoying *now* to give the past much consideration."

Having discussed the relationships between these entrepreneurs and their circles of families and friends, we asked them to tell us about the role that faith or spirituality plays in their lives. We asked also whether faith plays a part in their entrepreneurial endeavors, and when taking risks. We wanted to know whether they found solace or comfort in faith and spirituality. We specifically did not ask about religion, but about faith in themselves and their ability to take risks.

"It's very hard for me to separate my faith from who I am," David Neeleman said. "I can't tell you where the faith stops and I begin because it's so integral to my being and it so influences my thinking. I like to think I'm a good person just because I wanted to be good, not because I have some reward up in someplace that may or may not exist. I have a really strong belief that if you do the right thing, if you treat people well, you're going to live more happily. You're going to have more joy in your life and feel more fulfilled. I believe that, if you're a person who matters, if you're a person whom people look up to and respect, you're going to have a happier life. If you have some reward on the other side, that's cool too, but I think the rewards can be in this life for doing the right thing. Those things don't come easy. They come with a lot of sacrifice, but the sacrifice is well worth it because you'll have a family with a heart and a soul."

"I think life is like a mathematical equation," Wally Amos reflects. "If you change any part of a mathematical equation, then you change the answer. If you change any part of your life, then you don't know where you'd be. But I don't play the game of what would I be doing if I hadn't done this or that. It's immaterial."

When we asked what he would say about spirituality to people he was mentoring, he told us that his words from his experience would be to "believe in themselves, their abilities, and in a power greater than themselves. Whatever your belief, it is important to believe [in something]. You must be honest, have a good attitude, and give back to the community. I think that having faith, believing in yourself, and having a good attitude, are critical to anyone's success."

On the other hand, David Oreck doesn't feel that faith has played a role in his life of taking risks and being an entrepreneur. When we asked how he overcomes fear when taking major risks, he told us that he doesn't think you really *do* overcome the fear.

"I think you learn to live with it," he said. "You take your chances. It's just like when I was on bombing raids during the war. Anybody who said that he wasn't frightened was a liar. It's amazing how tight your jaw can get when someone is shooting at you from underneath. The fact is you deal with it. It's like stress. If you don't learn to deal with it and how to handle it, you let it overcome you. You can't be consumed by fear. There comes a point when you're simply resigned to what will be, will be. At that point, I give it everything I have, and I will continue to do this."

Confronting Failure

It is axiomatic that you can tell a lot about successful entrepreneurs from how they have dealt with ventures they have undertaken that were *not* successful. With that in mind, we pointedly asked them whether they had been confronted by failure, and how they dealt with it.

In general, we have seen that the truly successful deal with setbacks by redoubling their efforts. The old adage, which is still valuable even if it has been widely overused, states, "When the going gets tough, the tough get going."

As Ben Cohen told us, he felt as though he and Jerry were facing failure for most of the first ten years of their business. When this happened, their reaction was simply to work harder.

While all of the entrepreneurs with whom we spoke had achieved great success, many had also known defeat and disappointment.

> "I think there is a difference between tenacity and just hard work. I think that a lot of people don't have that. They are not tenacious, and they give up. I don't. I'm just stubborn."
>
> —David Oreck

People such as Jerry Baldwin, David Oreck, Wally Amos, and Jeff Taylor, as well as Kate and Andy Spade, are serial entrepreneurs who have been involved in multiple businesses during their careers. David Oreck, for example, has started, purchased, and/or grown more than a dozen different businesses through the years. Not all of their businesses have been as successful as they might have hoped, although all afforded valuable learning experiences.

Jerry Baldwin told us that one of his early failures in the coffee and tea business came in the 1970s. "When we were really young, there was a lot of opportunity, but we weren't very disciplined," he said. "In 1980, when Zev Siegel sold out, we had several discreet operations in a company that was probably doing a million dollars in sales. And one of them was a spiced flavored tea company. We developed a product line of flavored teas, and went out to sell them into supermarkets, not knowing what we were doing. We introduced our product in the same week that Lipton introduced theirs. They just kicked our butt. It probably took a year or more before our product got sold out and just went away. The lesson here is to *learn the competition*, not to necessarily run your business based on the competition, but to know what's happening and when."

We asked David Oreck whether he had ever had a business that has failed, and he told us candidly that he had "stubbed my toe here and there."

He went on to tell a story about a company that he owned that made grandfather clocks.

"I love clocks," he said. "We made a damn good clock, but shipping a long-cased clock and getting it there in one piece—when someone drops it off the back of his truck—just didn't work very well for us. I was very disappointed about this, and ultimately I had to close down the company. Hopefully you learn something by going through this sort of thing. I didn't let it stop me. I licked my wounds and carried on."

He added that he was quick to say it was a mistake and that it was *his* mistake. "I don't believe in blaming, and I'm very suspicious of people who constantly blame others," Oreck said. "I feel this is a great fault of many people. Whether it's their ego or whatever it is, they can't bring themselves to say, 'I made a mistake.' They have to scrounge around and find who to blame for it. Finally it turns out that the janitor is responsible. Admitting mistakes comes from having enjoyed enough success so that your ego is in place. Then you don't think you have any trouble saying that you made a mistake, or admitting that there is something that you don't know. You have to learn to say 'I don't know. I'm not sure what to do on that score. Let's find out.'"

Oreck explained that a key lesson in failure is not to let it cause you to give up: "I think there is a difference between tenacity and just hard work. I was tenacious and, frankly, I still am. I think that a lot of people don't have that. They are not tenacious, and they give up. I don't. I'm just stubborn."

As Andy Spade told us, he and Kate once "hit a major brick wall, but we just dug ourselves out, kept on going and kept on

> **"Making mistakes doesn't mean that what you did was a failure, or the wrong take. It was just a '*mis*-take.' You need to go back and do another take. In each take there is a lesson."**
>
> **—Wally Amos**

going. You regroup. You bring everyone together, and you talk about the problem, how it affects the people, and how best to solve it. You ask whether you're doing it intelligently, and whether you are making the right decisions. We talk with our group internally and work toward solving the issue, either by taking it on ourselves or by finding additional help. Then you just have to shake it off and move forward."

Often, we see calamity turn into opportunity with entrepreneurs. In our own business, in late 2005, we encountered several obstacles and lost a quarter of our business, plus some key people. However, we regrouped and had our best year ever in 2006. This was due to persistence and focusing on our clients' concerns, not our own.

"Making mistakes is a part of life," Wally Amos says. "Making mistakes doesn't mean that what you did was a failure, or the wrong take. It was just a '*mis*-take.' You need to go back and do another take. In each take there is a lesson. The idea is to learn from the experience, and not repeat the same mistake over and over again."

Analyzing his own reaction when things didn't go well, Amos candidly told us, "I lost my Famous Amos brand because I lost track of the importance of a team. I was disregarding my team. At one point, I thought that I was more important than the team. I got ahead of the team, rather than being a part of the team. As a result, I lost Famous Amos. No one took the company from me. When it happened, I realized that I would really have to look at myself, who I was, how I responded to life, and what I needed to do differently in the future. This was a wonderful growing process for me, but it will never happen again. I really believe good comes from everything, and every experience that you have comes to you to teach you something. If you don't get the lesson, then you're going to have the experience over and over again. This had been perhaps the biggest mistake I've ever made from a business perspective, but, it was one of the best things to ever happen to me because I learned so much. As a result, I was forced to be introspective, and to really look at who Wally Amos was and how I needed to handle myself and do business in the future."

Though Wally Amos lost control of his Famous Amos brand when he sold the company, he bounced back with Uncle Noname's Muffin Company. Started in 1994 in cooperation with his partner, Lou Avignone, a Famous Amos distributor, the company became Uncle Wally's Muffin Company in 1999.

"When I started Uncle Wally's Muffin Company, one of the first things I did was get a team of people, and then I let that team of people run the company," Amos told us. "The company is responsible, they're having great sales, and they're doing very well. I make a contribution based on my skills and on what I'm capable of doing."

Speaking from experience, Wally Amos had this to say: "It's really critical for each of us to look at what's happening in our lives. You want to take credit for all the good stuff, but when something bad happens you want to blame everybody else for what he or she is doing to you. The reality is that you always do it to yourself. No one ever does anything to you. You're the biggest culprit in your life. When you can take responsibility for everything that happens in your life, then you can fix those things that aren't working."

Sometimes lack of success is simply that, rather than out-and-out failure. As Jeff Taylor told us, "I think I've missed on successes more than I've had dominant failures. One of my biggest failures was that I started a second business, and I left my good people in my first business. If you don't take your good people with you, you will regret it. It is a difficult thing to leave your current business intact and start again. You never recapture the people and energy that you would have liked to have made the transition with you over into your new ideas."

"Failure is something that you're going to have throughout your life," David Neeleman said, explaining what he does if a particular strategy does not work for him. "My first business failed. I was in college and I started a little travel wholesale company. I was making money, so I dropped out of college to run it. I had a BMW, a house, and two kids. Then, the airline I was using went bankrupt and all the money of my customers went with them. I was out of business, and I felt like just giving up at that point."

Neeleman was co-founder, with June Morris, of the charter airline Morris Air. He served as executive vice president of Morris Air from 1984 to 1988, and as president from 1988 until Southwest Airlines acquired Morris Air for $130 million in 1993. He briefly remained on the executive planning committee at Southwest.

"When I was fired from Southwest, it was a very disappointing time for me because I had just sold my company. I had all the money I ever wanted, but I didn't have my job and I didn't have my company. I was miserable."

Using the analogy of "the tough get going," Neeleman decided to jump back in, telling himself that "I'm going to do it better than I did it before and I'm going to learn from this experience."

As he puts it, "I think it's not what happens to you in life, it's how you deal with adversity that really defines who you are. I've always tried to bounce back from the hard times, learn from the experience, and ask, 'How am I going to make sure a third-party company never causes me to go out of business again? How am I going to protect myself from that?'"

Jim Koch told us that he considers himself to have been lucky since he left Boston Consulting Group to start his company. He said that Boston Beer Company wasn't an overnight success, but that it has done well.

"One story that does stick with me is from the guy who was my mentor from BCG," Koch said, reflecting on the risks of business. "He had gone to General Electric, which was a client of mine. I was talking to him about what I wanted to do, and that I was going to leave and start this beer company. I told him that I knew it was a risk, but it was what I wanted to do. He told me, 'Jim you really shouldn't think of it as that risky. You're always going to be able to make a living. In fact I would sooner hire you with two years of a failed entrepreneurship on your resumé, than two more years of Boston Consulting Group.'"

As Koch puts it, "There is a big difference between actual risk and perceived risk. This was something I had to explain to people when I was teaching mountaineering. In mountaineering, when people learn to rappel over a cliff, you have to get them to walk backward over the edge. The perceived risk is quite high. The actual risk is trivial—you could hang a car on those ropes. Business is a

> "What you *do* speaks so loudly that I cannot hear what you *say*."
>
> —Ralph Waldo Emerson

lot like that. There are situations of high perceived risk. My going out and starting my own company had high perceived risk, but low actual risk. Even if it had failed, I would have been more hireable. On the other hand, staying in my fancy high-paid job at BCG was low perceived risk, but high actual risk. What if I got a big promotion and a bunch more money and was tempted to stay in a job that really wasn't right for me? Then I would have lost this chance!"

Mentoring

Mentoring is a key aspect of leadership. The developmental relationship between an accomplished leader and a less experienced member of the organization is seen as essential, not only for the growth of the individual being mentored, but also for the perpetuation of the organization itself. In business, mentoring grooms up-and-coming employees who are seen as possessing the potential to become leaders.

Mentoring has been part of organizational structures since antiquity. Indeed, the term "mentor" itself is derived from the name of the individual in Homer's *Odyssey* in whose guise the goddess Athena guides Telemachus through adversity. It is evident in the apprenticeship practices in the trades, and is perhaps best described by Ralph Waldo Emerson, who said: "What you *do* speaks so loudly that I cannot hear what you *say*."

"Being the example you want others to follow is important," Wally Amos said, citing the Emerson quote.

In our conversations with the entrepreneurs, many had comments on the subject of how they would mentor younger protégés. David Neeleman said he tells people not to undertake something on the scale of starting a new venture unless they have the passion.

"If you feel like it's something that consumes you, do it," he says. "If it's something that you want to do just because you don't want to work for somebody else, and you're trying to find something to do, *don't* do it. You should just go work for somebody else, because being an entrepreneur is a tough job. It's fraught with failures."

When asked what thoughts he would share with someone whom he was mentoring, Jim Koch said that he or she should realize there is nothing that we do that we cannot improve.

"It's just part of the culture that we're never satisfied with what we did yesterday," he said. "If you ask me, it's not about throwing massive financial resources at it. It's about ideas and culture and software, not hardware. I wrote an article in *The New York Times* a couple of years ago about what I had learned when I was an Outward Bound instructor. I called it my 'string theory.' If you gave your group plenty of string before they went out for their 28 days in the wilderness, they would come back with less than they needed because they had started with too much. They had wasted a resource that appeared abundant, and ended up short. If you gave them too little, they would come back with plenty because they rationed their resources more carefully. The lesson from this in an entrepreneurial environment within a small company is that attitude and culture are an effective substitute for resources."

Koch is well known for his "restless dissatisfaction with the status quo," so we asked him to give us a mentoring example of something that demonstrates this fact.

"As I have said, I taste every batch of beer that we brew, so a couple times a week our director of brewing gets messages from me about specific batches," Koch explained. "I *ask* him why this batch was good, or why the aroma was a little suppressed in another one. There is constant poking at these things. I keep little sticky notes in my pocket so that as things occur to me, I can pull one out."

"You're not driven only by what your life should be," Andy Spade said. "You have to strategize your business, but you have to strategize your life *before* you strategize your business. What do you want your life to look like? What kind of day do you want to have? What time do you want to wake up? Where do you want to live? Do you want to be in a sunny environment or not a sunny environment? What kind of people do you want to work with? My friend Hugo said 'I don't want a lot of people reporting to me, I want to make sure I'm not doing something that demands a lot of staff.'"

Spade went on to say that, when he started in business, he was told that the competition would "chew you up and spit you out. People in this industry are as tough as nails and they're going to do that to you."

Today, looking back on this, he said: "I think every industry is like this to some degree. I'd rather follow my personal path and let the business be a by-product of that. We could focus exclusively on handbags and probably do very well, but we had a bigger vision than that and it wouldn't be as challenging."

It is evident from our interviews that these distinguished entrepreneurs are markedly diverse in their leadership traits. It is also clear that their distinctive styles and personalities transcend external communications and customer relations to greatly impact each corporation's culture. This is not to say that a consistent and remarkable brand experience and the company's commitment to keeping its brand promise means that today's most successful business leaders offer the ideal work environment. While some have achieved this, many others work toward constant improvement.

As an appropriate means of summarizing this chapter on "Leadership Qualities and Beliefs", I turn to my personal and revealing discussion with Jerry Baldwin, co-founder of Starbucks and principal of Peet's Coffee. He points out, "There is a difference between being and becoming. From my experience, I know philosophically that we will never be perfect, but we always strive to *become* perfect. So there is a sense of continuous improvement and continuous striving. To me, that defines a personal philosophy as well as a business and leadership philosophy. It's continuous learning."

As we have seen in this chapter, each of the entrepreneurs whom we interviewed possesses a different leadership style, but there are common characteristics.

- The human-resources practices of these entrepreneurs are aligned with their cultures of authenticity.

- Staff reviews should occur often so as to avoid surprises.

- These business leaders hire talented people based primarily on their attitudes and personalities.

- Healthy conflict and questioning of the status quo can be positive.

- The overwhelming majority of these business leaders believe that accountability is essential for success.

- Everyone agrees that meetings must be productive, to-the-point, and focused.

- Showing vulnerability can communicate sincerity and build trust.

- Failure may mean you are on the brink of success beyond your wildest imagination.

Chapter 8:
Shared Insights and Experiences

In the previous chapter, we got personal. We probed the individual leadership and management philosophies of these entrepreneurs. We asked them how they dealt with employee issues and how entrepreneurs balanced their business and personal lives. We asked them how they overcame adversity and what lessons they had learned from their failures.

In this chapter, we use the words of these entrepreneurs to provide additional lessons that you can apply to build your own "better mousetrap."

Is There a Better Mousetrap?

The well-known and often repeated "mousetrap" analogy comes from the old adage that states "Build a better mousetrap and the world will beat a path to your door." The meaning is that customers are attracted to a product or service that is an improvement over existing products or services in the same category—and that learning how to do it is one giant step on the road to success.

Attributed to a quotation from Ralph Waldo Emerson, writing in his journal in 1855, the quotation may actually have been written in 1889 by Sarah S.B. Yule and Mary S. Keene, who were

> "The *better* mousetrap is really illusive because the basic mousetrap still works best. To say that you've built a *better* mousetrap is kind of an oxymoron."
>
> —Jeff Taylor

paraphrasing Emerson when they wrote "If a man can write a better book, preach a better sermon, or make a better mousetrap than his neighbor, though he build his house in the woods, the world will make a beaten path to his door."

In any case, the phrase has become a widely quoted, and almost universally accepted, axiom in the field of marketing. It tells us that the marketplace will be responsive to quality.

Emerson actually used the examples of "better chairs or knives, crucibles or church organs" rather than mousetraps, but the mousetrap analogy is more illustrative. This is so because the current mousetrap design has been used for more than a century without significant change. This means that a "better mousetrap," if it were to be built, would indeed be a revolutionary product. As Jeff Taylor points out, "The *better* mousetrap is really elusive because the basic mousetrap still works best. To say that you've built a *better* mousetrap is kind of an oxymoron."

Taylor observed, "Today, a lot of the innovation is not about mousetrap building—it's about what color to paint the mousetrap. It's about how you get it in front of people to show how impressive the spring is, and about your ability to market and sell that mousetrap. If you look at Monster, our jobs business is still 50 percent of our business, and our resumé business is 30 percent. These two products were in development as early as 1993, so for more than a decade, we've been pressing the accelerator on how to get these two products to more and more companies, and to more and more job seekers."

Elaborating on the smaller examples of the spring and the color of the trap, Taylor said that for him, creating brand awareness was a fundamental "spring."

"Developing your aided and unaided brand awareness is an art, not a science," he says. "It was a long-term effort to get us to the place where nine out of ten adults working in the United States know what Monster is. There are some brands that go through their entire life cycle without anyone's knowing what they really are."

When we asked Gary Hirshberg how he had tried to build his better mousetrap, he replied by saying: "First I'll explain what the mousetrap *is* that I'm trying to build, and I would use the present tense not the past. This is because I think we're always at the starting line. This is a continuous improvement process–you're never done. Conventional consumer products have the same basic algorithm that you are always trying to make the product as cheap as you possibly can."

He went on to cite the examples of Pepsi Cola and Coca Cola, and how they build their existing, and essentially unchanging, mousetraps: "They use sugar water, corn-syrup solids and some coloring. There is nothing really cheaper than that. There is no nutritional value, no food, and no meaning. The point of this is that you can take the huge gross margins that are left over to purchase advertising and to buy media. Of course, in examples involving advertising, you use the media to get an 'awareness trial' and, ultimately, you hope, loyalty."

As Hirshberg suggests, there is a baseline level of product

> "So the mousetrap that we've been trying to build is one that does not depend on advertising, at least not in the conventional sense. It's one that communicates *authenticity*—a value proposition to the consumer so that he or she can relate to us as humans, not as some faceless, anonymous corporation."
>
> —Gary Hirshberg

quality in every product category, and that competing with that baseline often involves building a better advertising campaign rather than building a better mousetrap.

"If you believe as I do, that a consumable item that goes into a yogurt container should be something edible—as radical as that notion may be—then you right away buy into the idea that you're not going to cut costs," he explains. "In my case, I'm trying to feed people not only healthy food and nutritious food, but I'm also trying to feed the farmers that sustain us. I'm trying to rebuild the food system and a supply chain. By definition, this means that my gross margins are at a disadvantage to my competitors, and this means that I can't afford advertising. However, as you can see, our business has grown north of 23 percent for over a dozen straight years. Recently, we grew 45 percent in a category that has traditionally grown between five and eight percent. I'm now the number three yogurt brand nationally, and the number one organic yogurt brand globally."

This leads to Hirshberg's belief that building a better advertising campaign can and should be secondary to building a better mousetrap.

"So the mousetrap that we've been trying to build is one that does not depend on advertising, at least not in the conventional sense. It's one that communicates *authenticity*—a value proposition to the consumer so that he or she can relate to us as humans, not as some faceless, anonymous corporation. Our consumers can relate to us as the people who are behind the product, and therefore as the people who are committed to their needs as part of a *solutions* company, not just a yogurt company. How have I tried to build it? For the first eight years, I had to prove this hypothesis without really having any role models in business. My father and grand-father were shoe manufacturers who owned shoe factories. They obviously were severe polluters, but I don't fault them for that. Back in their era, there was a concept known as 'away,' in which you could ship waste away to somewhere else—into rivers or the air. On the other hand, like we try to do, they were also sustaining whole communities. Of course, we have watched their industry, and the communities it supported, become decimated."

Hirshberg explained that the Stonyfield Farm mousetrap is as much a system of values as it is a brand of yogurt which, as we now can see, emanates from authenticity: "The mousetrap that I've tried to build is one where we are partners in communicating a *value system* to the consumers. To accomplish this, we retrain employees and professionals who come from the consumer-product world where they have been used to relying on the power of advertising. Here, they can think differently. It's been a bit more of an educational odyssey than a business odyssey, as we've attempted to show all of the stake-holders in this process that, if we band together, we can essentially create a better world for all."

When we asked Ben Cohen how he strived to build a better

mousetrap to improve the way he and Jerry Greenfield did business, he told us, "We were constantly trying to improve. We were in the mode of continuous improvement before continuous improvement came into vogue. We were some of the early pioneers in the world of continuous improvement. It's just a little personality quirk of mine that I'm never satisfied with what I have. I want only what I don't have."

Jerry Greenfield continued the thought by explaining that, for Ben, the mousetraps were the ice cream flavors.

"I used to make the ice cream, but Ben was the creator of the different flavors," Jerry said. "He was in charge of quality improvement, so no matter what I made, Ben would say 'this is really great, but can't we make the chunks bigger or can't we make the flavor a little stronger?' It was great. We started as a homemade-ice-cream parlor and, when you make homemade ice cream, you're doing it by hand, so you can pretty much make things any way you want. If you wanted to chop a little bigger, you just do it by hand."

He went on to explain that the real challenge came when Ben and Jerry started to manufacture on a much larger scale.

"None of the equipment was designed to make ice cream the way we wanted to do it. Ice cream was typically made in a way that was easy for the machinery. It's not necessarily what the people want, but it's what the machines could make. Ben was always pushing us to modify the equipment and change things so that we could make ice cream the way we wanted, as opposed to what the machinery wanted to make."

David Neeleman is also committed to continual improvement and innovation as the key to the better mousetrap. He told us that in the airline business, you can't stand still.

"This is a difference of opinion that I had with Southwest Airlines. They had become prisoners of their own success. They had one business model that worked so well they were very hesitant to change anything. Their system of first-come, first-served seating worked fine when they were flying in a market such as intra-Texas, but not when they're flying from Baltimore to Oakland. You don't even know if you're going to sit next to your wife with whom you've been planning this trip for six months, or not. That can be stressful. Also, at Southwest, any kind of in-flight entertainment is just taboo. They don't want to do any of it because it might affect their operation. What if General Electric had continued to make only light bulbs? They would've been in trouble, and probably wouldn't be in business today. You have to be able to adapt and change as the environment that you're in changes. You need to be able to change your business model when it doesn't seem to be working."

Having said this, Neeleman does not advocate that we should dilute our focus—just adapt to change and be aware of our customers' sometimes unspoken needs. Describing Southwest as an airline that continually rolls out the same mousetrap—albeit a quality mousetrap—Neeleman tells us what sets JetBlue apart. Among the better mousetraps pioneered by JetBlue have been the E-Ticket and live in-flight television. In 2006, the authoritative trade magazine *Air Transport World* named JetBlue Airways as the winner of its Passenger Service Award, citing innovations that included seat back television programming from Florida-based LiveTV. The publication noted that JetBlue "has changed passenger perceptions and raised expectations of what a budget airline can and should be."

Said David Neeleman, "You need to be able to add new features as technology becomes available. It was such an oddity to get aboard and see live television that nobody thought was even possible. The minute we saw that it *was* possible, we said, 'That's something we want.' Nothing could dissuade us from doing it. It turned out to be a huge success. We decided to expand and go to 36 channels and include movie options. Then we heard about XM Satellite Radio, and we thought that maybe some people would like to be listening to some jazz as they cruise across the country."

As for the idea of E-Ticket travel, Neeleman said he wondered: "Why do you have to require people to bring these ridiculous documents with them when you can just have a confirmation number? They don't need to bring tickets. Innovations like this have changed our industry."

"I still taste a bottle of every batch of Sam Adams," Jim Koch told us, giving examples of how he is always on edge, constantly looking for ways to improve. "I'm always tasting it, thinking about it, and trying to decide whether there's anything I could have done better with the batch. Even now, I'm staying pretty close to the actual brewing, and there are always little opportunities that present themselves. Recently, I was in Germany selecting hops, when we started talking to their technical people about other ways to store the hops. Hops are actually very delicate flowers, and you're trying to preserve their aromatic and their spice qualities. We were working on ways of keeping them colder, and creating a cold chain all the way from the farm to the brewery."

Of this continual quest for a better mousetrap, Koch mentioned: "Somebody who works here had a nice phrase. When talking about the general attitude at Sam Adams, he said there is a 'restlessness of dissatisfaction with the status quo that's part of the culture.' I thought that was a nice phrase because it's true."

In our public relations business, we call this "a healthy degree of paranoia," to ensure that our team realizes the "what have you done for me lately" client mindset. This is very persuasive; therefore, it has forced us to develop reporting and systems to ensure that our clients *always* know what we are doing on their behalf and that they *always* know the results.

Like many entrepreneurs, Bobbi Brown sees the search for the better mousetrap as a matter of being constantly in motion, constantly on the lookout for innovation.

"I am always thinking we can do better," she told us. "Getting the right people in place is probably the most important element for this innovation or improvement."

For Andy and Kate Spade, the mousetraps were Kate's remarkable fabric handbags that appeared in the market when the fashion leaders were leading with leather.

"I think I was the one who suggested that we start with handbags," Andy Spade explained. "The reason was because of Kate's experience. We had talked about starting an advertising agency, which is my background, but we decided that I'd keep my day job at Chiat Day to pay our overhead and help with the start-up costs while she started Kate Spade. For the first two years, I worked with her on weekends and evenings."

He went on to describe how he and Kate staked out a market niche. In this niche, the better mousetrap was a fabric bag that made its appearance at a time when the fashion industry largely ignored fabric bags.

"Kate and I believe we were the first on this scale to exclusively do fabric bags," he says. "We started the business when handbags were not as relevant in society and culture as they are today. If

> **"I think that it is necessary to improve. It's not necessarily that I'm always looking for a new mousetrap, but I *always* want to be known for excellence."**
>
> **—Wally Amos**

you look back to the early 1990s, I think that the only other company doing fabric bags was Prada. They did a black rayon bag. What has continued to really differentiate us is our use of innovative fabrics and prints. Kate used a lot of ready-to-wear fabrics, which weren't being used at the time. Meanwhile, Coach was an exclusively leather handbag company. Dooney and Burke was all leather, and their products were kind of stiff, not soft and lightweight. That was a big part. Design was a big part, and so was the fact that we had a story. People could relate to Kate. She was a *real* person. It wasn't just a label; there was a human component to it. The product innovation was truly authentic, and it carved out a niche in the market."

Andy confirmed that the notion of building a better mousetrap analogy has played an important part in growing their business beyond handbags. "Yes, it has," he told us. "I think since the day we started, we've been looking at new ways to do things within the categories in which we live. We never thought of ourselves as the 'handbag company;' we thought of ourselves as a design company. We try to infuse a lot of personality into what we do."

Knowing that Wally Amos is committed to growing personally as an individual, we asked him how, in terms of his business, he strives for improvement and growth, and to create his better mousetrap.

"I think that it is necessary to improve," he said. "It's not necessarily that I'm always looking for a new mousetrap, but I *always* want to be known for excellence. I've been in the business for 30 years, and I've never had anything negative written about me. I've lived my life in a manner so as to solicit that type of response from people. As long as you do that, you'll always advance and improve. Here I am, 30 years later, starting another cookie company with a new concept built around two chocolate chip cookie dolls. We're selling cookies, T-shirts, dolls, and baseball caps. More important than the products we're selling, is that the Chip and Cookie brand is promoting reading. When I started Famous Amos, we were promoting literacy, too. The cornerstone of this new business is promoting the "Read Aloud Foundation," and we're contributing ten percent of our earnings to the foundation. We have a small section in our store where anyone can read to kids." As with others we've interviewed, Amos's authentic approach is about more than just profits. There are underlying passions, issues, missions and visions by which these leaders become energized.

David Oreck agrees that, as he was building his company, he was always looking to build a better mousetrap, and that he was constantly changing as he did so. As with Neeleman, he has always found that change is a challenge, but that standing still is a grave mistake.

With Thomas Friedman's "flattening of the world" concept, the United States and other national economies, as well as the global economy, are inter-related and continually changing. Therefore, anticipating change, and adapting and innovating are the essential ingredients of continued success.

"If you do as I did," Oreck continues, "if you start with nothing and struggle, you realize that it's not only a struggle the first day, it's also a struggle, in the first year and in the tenth year. It's

> "Most certainly you have to be prepared for change. Therefore, you have to be on top of the business, and you have to look for little things before they get to be big things."
>
> —David Oreck

one thing to start something if you have a bunch of stockholders who are funding the deal, but that wasn't the case with me. You have to be on top of your business all the time, and it's a changing thing, a moving stream. Certain fundamentals, of course, are constant, but the greatest constant in business is change. There are certain fundamentals you work with, but basically the business changes. All the small retailers of televisions and appliances are gone. I owned the RCA wholesale distributorship in New Orleans covering Louisiana, Mississippi, and Houston. Virtually all of those dealers that we dealt with are gone, and that's true all over the country."

"The fear of the unknown and the uncertainties keep you constantly on your toes," Oreck said when we asked him whether he fears change. "Most certainly you have to be prepared for change. Therefore, you have to be on top of the business, and you have to look for little things before they get to be big things."

He explained that he welcomed change because he saw opportunity even in adversity. He quoted Britain's wartime prime minister, Sir Winston Churchill, who said "A pessimist sees the difficulty in every opportunity; an optimist sees the opportunity in every difficulty."

"When I started in my business career, I opened all of the mail," he said, moving to illustrate Churchill's idea. "Without exception, every single letter of complaint I received got an answer. I think to grow, you have to be on top of things, and pay attention. Look for signs, so you can be ahead of the game, so that you're not blind-sided when something comes up. I had a problem not long ago involving a product that we were buying from someone else that turned out to be defective. We found the problem, and in examining it carefully, we found the issue that caused the problem. It was the failure of a certain electronic component. What I'm getting at, is that we found the basic defect. *Why* it failed was what mattered. If you have the answer to that, then you can determine whether it is an isolated failure of a component part, or something really fundamental that makes a huge difference. As quickly as you discover a product defect, you're looking at an *opportunity.*"

When we asked him whether he would recommend a vertical operation such as he has built into his business, Oreck told us, "It can be more difficult, and it certainly places financial burdens on you that you wouldn't otherwise have."

Yet he explained that it also has obvious advantages: "Logistics are a little easier and, if you've got a problem, you can fix it quickly. For example, I don't have to go to China if I want to change something. I pick up the telephone and an hour later it's affected. The following day, the product comes off the line and it has that change. In fact, we print our own manuals and information sheets at the factory, so if there's a change we can produce new printed materials."

A big part of learning from the experience of those who have built better mousetraps in the past is knowing what they would have done differently to have made the process go faster or more smoothly. For most of the entrepreneurs with whom we spoke,

They want their total corporate image, and the image of their brand, to be as much about their system of values as it is about the tangible product that they put on the shelf. This is what distinguishes *authentic* entrepreneurs and their *authentic* brands from the "Brand Xs" of the world.

their reflecting back on how the mousetraps might have been made better came down to relatively concise comments. Gary Hirshberg recalled, "Every entrepreneur has a tendency to set revenue projections too *high*, and cost projections too *low*. The result for us was a lot more dilution than we probably would have taken if we'd been a little bit more realistic."

David Neeleman was not joking when he replied: "What one thing would I do differently? I'd hedge more fuel. I'd hedge for 20 years. I'd have prepaid fuel for as long as I could!"

Jeff Taylor, recalling that he sold Monster.com relatively early in the process, told us: "If I had the choice again, I still would have sold when I did, but I would have probably tried to command the control of a few more areas. I sold it to an entrepreneur, and there were also a few other entrepreneurs in the house. Over time, this created an extremely successful partnership, but it was also a tiny bit crowded."

Andy Spade told us that one thing he and Kate would have done is to have worked on their other ideas outside of the framework of their existing business.

"Kate said the only reason I did the handbag was as an excuse for everything else I wanted to do," he laughed. "I was bringing up a lot of the ideas and actually bringing them into this business. I had a lot of passions, and I figured out ways for them to become brand extensions. The Jack Spade brand was an example, as was a hobby shop called 'Hobby Dashery,' for clothing and toys that I like. I learned a lot through this business because I've been surrounded by a lot of great people, but I do wish I had spent 25 percent of my time pursuing other things."

David Oreck told us that what he would have done differently is to have done it all sooner, instead of waiting until he was 40 to start his first business. "Young people have got time to make mistakes," he explained. "You shouldn't be afraid to make a mistake. You shouldn't be afraid of being fired. They might be doing you a favor."

Mission Statements

Just as the mousetrap analogy illustrates a business leader's commitment to constant improvement, and the consumers' responsiveness to the quality of a product, it is true that today's entrepreneurs also want consumers to be responsive to their personal and corporate value systems and messages. As we've discussed in our chapter on doing good to do well, companies today have a commitment to being an important part of their community and of society in general. They want their total corporate image, and the image of their brand, to be as much about their system of values as it is about the tangible product that they put on the shelf. This is what distinguishes *authentic* entrepreneurs and their *authentic* brands from the "Brand Xs" of the world.

For this reason, companies now put a great deal of emphasis on both creating and living their mission statements. However, as Jim Collins and Jerry Porras point out in *Built to Last: Successful Habits of Visionary Companies*, the most successful companies put more emphasis on living their vision than drafting their statements.

"The visionary companies attained their stature not so much because they made visionary pronouncements (although they often did make such pronouncements)," Collins and Porras write. "Nor did they rise to greatness because they wrote one of the vision, values, purpose, mission, or aspiration statements that have become popular in management today (although they wrote such statements more frequently than the comparison companies and decades before it became fashionable). Creating a statement can be a helpful step in building a visionary company, but it is only one of thousands of steps in a never-ending process of expressing the fundamental characteristics we identified across the visionary companies."

In our conversations, we asked the entrepreneurs not so much to recite their mission statements, but to relate to us what importance their mission statements play in their companies' operations.

The commitment to values was very much in evidence at Ben & Jerry's. When asked about the mission statement that he and Ben Cohen crafted, Jerry Greenfield told us, "I think ours is a little different from most. Most business mission statements talk about creating great products, satisfying your customers' needs and exceeding expectations. Delighting your customers is a wonderful thing to do. What was unusual about our mission statement was that we talked about having a three-part mission: a product mission, which would include incredibly high-quality ice cream; an economic mission, which talked about a fair return for our investors or stakeholders; and then we also talked about a social mission for the company. That is the part that was different from most other businesses. We were very explicit that it was very important to the other parts of the mission. They were all interrelated."

If Ben & Jerry's Homemade was an early proponent of adopting a social-consciousness component to its mission statement, they were by no means alone. Most of the entrepreneurs with whom we spoke when we were developing this book also felt this way.

As with Ben & Jerry's, Stonyfield Farm is a company with a strong social responsibility mission. With this in mind, we asked Gary Hirshberg how he communicates this to his employees so that it is clear internally on an ongoing basis.

> **"Most companies don't solve something as interesting as world hunger, but you can be doing something that is really meaningful. The words you use in your 'mission vision values' are less important than just harnessing the culture that will be created automatically if you're doing good work."**
>
> **—Jeff Taylor**

"This is an enormous challenge and opportunity," he told us. "The answer is that we never do it well enough—or enough, period. Traditionally we have had twice-annual whole-staff meetings, which continue even now that it's spread into two plants on each coast. These meetings are my opportunity to sit in front of my folks and set up a presentation that will leave no doubt as to the depth of our mission and our commitment. We've converted a lot of people into organic believers here. We have an internal newsletter and intranet. Our reward system is structured around encouraging understanding of the mission. We just don't throw lunches when we break a record, we have *organic* lunches, and we have organic-education breakfasts. If a group of Stonyfield employees want to make a commitment, the company will match that commitment. Let me just say bluntly that this job is never, never complete."

"I think that it is important for a company to solve some problems—such as world hunger, to use as one example," Jeff Taylor told us. "Most companies don't solve something as interesting as world hunger, but you can be doing something that is really meaningful. The words you use in your 'mission vision values' are less important than just harnessing the culture that will be created automatically if you're doing good work."

Wally Amos agrees with Taylor that, if channeled properly, social responsibility grows organically from within an organization.

"My mission statement is helping employees and customers feel good about themselves," Amos told us. He has always been known for conveying his personal mission statement with his employees as a business person, and as a human being. He then reinforces it through regular emails, business cards which reinforce his personal mission, and with his website, WallyAmos.com.

"I don't think of myself as the president or CEO. From a business point of view," Amos explained, "I feel I'm 'a messenger of inspirations.' I want to inspire people. I want everyone in the organization to inspire people and to be inspired. If we can create an environment of enthusiasm and strong attitude within the store, then people will look forward to visiting us. This adds a little bonus. It differentiates us from everyone else. If there is a high level of enthusiasm, and good customer service, people will feel that they're important when they come into our stores."

Setting goals that include a high level of enthusiasm among employees, and good customer service, result in a retail consumer experience that is not contrived. It is genuine and *authentic*.

Jerry Baldwin told us that he wrote the Peet's mission statement in the 1980s, communicating it by putting it on the walls of stores, and by actively talking about it.

"One of the things about mission statements is that they should be short, about 25 words," he explained. "The idea in communicating it was to make it simple enough so that everyone could use it as a touchstone. I would meet with each class that we were training to be managers, and spend an hour talking about our values, and how to manage and respond to them. The most important message is show, don't tell. Don't say it, *do* it!"

The Spades told us that they have placed a great deal of importance on their mission statement since the day they started.

"One of the things we do is to manifest our passion in our mission statement," Kate explained. "We always wanted to have a nice, successful business, but at the same time, we always thought of ourselves as simply creative, intelligent *people*. We didn't set out to be known as savvy business people. That was never my goal in life. Our goal was to be really smart, curious, creative, and fair in business. I want to have a business that is successful, but wouldn't compromise the culture of the company for the success of the company. That may be a bad business decision, but we work here every day. We give out the etiquette book that we've published within the company. We have an orientation video that speaks to the idea of being smart *and* respectful in business. It isn't soft. It's actually a great business tool that helps to recruit people. People want to work for nice people. I think of this as a strategic tool, rather than just a

> "I get so wrapped up in the business. I just really want perfection all the time, and it's really hard to have perfection in this business."
>
> —David Neeleman

soft kind of fuzzy thing that you do because you want everyone to be nice. We built in style and graciousness."

Andy Spade added that he and Kate talk about these matters in public, and have written articles on how very important it is to make their company an "interesting place."

"I think that being gracious in life is essential," he continued. "If you look around, there are people whom you respect, people whom you want to be around. Jackie Onassis had it, and all of the greats had it. Our etiquette policy tells people internally and externally how to act, and it helps designers think about what to make, and it helps architects understand how to design space. It even tells the receptionist how to get coffee in the appropriate way. Gracious is universal. It's bigger than hip, sexy, or edgy. This is all part of our vision."

"We don't have a 'mission statement' as such," Neeleman said. "We have our five core values, which are safety, caring, fun, integrity, and passion. We call our employees 'crewmembers,' to make them feel like they're all part of a team. We don't call our customers 'passengers' either. Nobody wants to hear the word 'passenger'. We did some surveying recently, as we do every year, and on the question of how JetBlue values its customers, 96 percent of our people checked the highest box that they could. Our customers know that they are important to us. They know that we are constantly striving to *speak to their intelligence*. It's the same thing with our suppliers and vendors. We don't use those words. We use 'business partners.' It's also important to set an attitude in the nomenclature. I know talk is cheap, but it does reinforce the fact that customers really are important to us."

Can You Take the Business Too Seriously?

Keeping things in proper perspective is essential in business, but can you take yourself or your business *too* seriously? Jim Koch told us that he takes the beer seriously, but he doesn't want to take himself seriously. Both Ben Cohen and Jerry Greenfield told us that they'd never been accused of taking their business too seriously. Ben said that he had been accused of working too hard or spending too much time on it, but never of taking it too seriously.

"Only from my husband, not from anyone else," Bobbi Brown laughed when we asked if she had ever been accused of taking her business too seriously. "If anything, I've been accused of probably the opposite."

Jeff Taylor told us: "If anything, I've been accused of a *reverence*. I think that one of the skills I have developed along the way is the ability to be a chameleon in terms of knowing when it's time to step out and create a big moment—and when its time to kind of step back inside and make sure you run a good, fundamental company. I've had more quiet success in stepping back inside and making sure the company is run well in difficult times."

"I get so wrapped up in the business," David Neeleman explained, sharing his thoughts on keeping things in perspective. "I just really want perfection all the time, and it's really hard to have perfection in this business. I get really down if we're having a really bad day, a day when the flights are running late or getting cancelled. I think I suffer more than the customers who are on those flights because I really do not like to disappoint people. I just have to realize that as long as people are safe, I just have to relax."

"I'm not serious, but I *am* responsible," Wally Amos says. "I think there's a big difference between being serious and being responsible. Serious people often seem rigid, and this can make matters worse. Serious people can't have fun, but you can be responsible and have fun. I think it's important to have fun. Why wake up if you aren't going to enjoy life? Too many people go to jobs that they hate because it's the only thing they can do. They have to make a dollar, but who ever said you couldn't create an income doing what you love?"

When we asked Gary Hirshberg whether he had ever been accused of taking Stonyfield Farm too seriously, his immediate reaction was, "Oh, not to my face."

In a less whimsical vein, he added that, in the early days of the business, he had to take it very seriously.

"We went nine years before we made our first profit," he said, "so, needless to say, I had a lot of sleepless nights through that period. I don't think that I could have cut myself slack, because through most of that period I could not sleep. We took the company through some very rough losses, but, since we turned the corner, I've never really lost sleep over business."

Having said that, Hirshberg explained what to him is the authentic bottom line. "The real answer that I want to offer to your question is that business is the means to the end for me. And the end is not about making money, although I've created a lot of millionaires, and I've certainly made myself and my family a hefty fortune. The end for me is that the planet is in deep trouble. We are watching the end of the fossil fuel era as we speak, and the aftermath of Hurricane Katrina. Toxification and climate change and depletion of every known natural resource are now predicted for mid-century. Katrina has a different name, and this is global warming."

Referencing his background in science, he went on to explain to us what he really does take seriously. "I've been trained in climate change; I have no illusions about this. Back in the early 1970s, my professors laid out a very clear global climate model, showing that, somewhere around the early part of the twenty-first century, we are going to have hotter hots, colder colds, and much more severe storms. We see the ferocity of storms intensifying, and I don't think our civilization has a clue to what is in store. This is our future. I believe that business and commerce are what got us into this mess, and I also believe that commerce is going to be needed to get us out. I suppose people who don't share my somewhat dire views of the state of the planet might accuse me of taking it *too* seriously, but I don't think that is possible."

Like Gary Hirshberg, David Oreck redirected the question to what he really does take seriously, replying "I am a workaholic, and as far as being accused of that, I'd say that the only person who would accuse a hard worker of working too hard is someone who doesn't work all that hard. I have never worked for money per se, not that I have objected to it or anything of the sort, but that was not the motivator. My motivator is to be good at what I was doing, even if a lot of people thought I was an SOB along the way. My concern was that I wanted their *respect*. Like Rodney Dangerfield, I wanted their respect and the satisfaction of knowing that I did it, and that I did it very well."

Oreck mirrors other authentic brand-builders with his ancillary motives. As previously referenced, along with our other entrepreneurs, it is not just about the money for him. This greater purpose is about creating brands that resonate with people.

The Importance of Education

Among the basics of success in any business, or indeed in virtually any endeavor, is education. For the most part, the entrepreneurs we interviewed for this book, even those who never finished college, told us that they strongly believe in higher education. As Jeff Taylor says, "If you have the capacity and the capability, you are better off to get your traditional schooling done in the traditional time frame. That said, what is traditional schooling and a traditional time frame? I think it's a lot easier to go to college when you are between 18 and 22 than it is to go back when you're 39."

Taylor, however, was not one who was able to pick up his undergraduate degree when he was in his early twenties. He cites the fact that not everyone learns in the same way.

"I just didn't learn very well in a traditional book setting," Taylor told us. "I'm more of a hands-on learner. I actually went back to school and finished my undergraduate degree at the University of Massachusetts when I was 40. So it took me 23 years, but I did it. I actually went to Harvard Business School *before* I went back and finished my undergraduate degree. I did the three-year Owner/President Management (OPM) certificate program at Harvard, so I went in the opposite direction. When I graduated from UMASS with an undergraduate degree in May 2001, my son asked me, 'what are you going to do now?' I really believe in being a learning executive."

The OPM Program that Taylor attended was created by the Harvard Business school specifically for entrepreneurial business leaders, including "senior executives with a significant equity stake in their company" to provide tools, frameworks, and a global network to help executives advance their businesses. According to the school, "Participants gain new insights and proven strategies for sustainable success… [They] learn to assess their company's position, develop long-term strategies for change, and create action plans."

Andy Spade told us that he and Kate are like the many people who value the cultural coming of age that is part of the college experience, as well as the actual course work. "I wouldn't jump into the business world or any other professional capacity early," Andy says. "Kate and I enjoyed our college years. We say, don't be in a hurry. It's something you can't replace. You'll never get that time back. All of the life experiences from the college years actually informed us a lot. I think of the courses, and everyone I surrounded myself with. One thing I remember was an advertising course that was actually very inspiring. It showed me that you could get paid for thinking of ideas!"

While some of the entrepreneurs with whom we spoke are strong believers in the content of higher education—that which you learn in school—Jerry Baldwin thinks of college as intrinsically important for the sake of the experience. "I do think that the college years are a valuable time for young people. My grades weren't particularly good, but I learned a lot about myself and about life. You can't predict where you're going to get your inspiration as an entrepreneur though. It just kind of happens. My advice, which is probably conventional for my time, is to get broadly educated

> "To me, an entrepreneur is someone who would be equally happy in more than one business. A lot of people are serial entrepreneurs. They build one up, sell it off, and go on to the next."
>
> —Jerry Baldwin

rather than specifically educated."

Baldwin went on to say that he never thought of himself as an entrepreneur in the business school sense: "To me, the distinction that I made—when I bothered to make one—was that entrepreneurs, especially business school graduates in the 1980s, had learned to analyze opportunities. But we didn't do any of that. We tried lots of different ideas and opening a coffee store was just one more idea. Business plan? I didn't know what a business plan was. After the business got going, we tried to figure out what to do with it. I borrowed money from my sister, Gordon Bowker put up his own money, and we borrowed some from the bank. Our first presentation to the bankers was on a single page, and it didn't even have a balance sheet. You couldn't get a car loan with that sheet of paper today. There wasn't a business sense to it. It was three guys who opened a coffee store, and then figured out what to do next."

He went on to describe what he thought an entrepreneur is: "To me, an entrepreneur is someone who would be equally happy in more than one business. A lot of people are serial entrepreneurs. They build one up, sell it off, and go on to the next. In my case, there probably are any number of things I could have been interested in, but obviously you can tell from my longevity in the coffee business that I wasn't so eager to go on to the next one."

Bobbi Brown told us that her experience in school was like

that of many of us who excelled in certain things, but felt ourselves unsuited for other classes.

"I did very well in classes like art, history, or things I could learn visually," Bobbi says. "I had a history class where the teacher led us to make visualizations instead of sitting there reading books. I got to use my creativity and I learned so much about government. In other classes like algebra or biology, if I got Cs, it was a miracle. Ironically, I think it's helped me because now I'm almost overcompensating for things I didn't learn, and I've become a bigger reader. Learning never stops. I would certainly tell people to be open to learning. I believe in being a sponge."

Sometimes it is hard for someone who has become successful as an entrepreneur without a college degree to speak of the importance of a college education, but he or she does. David Neeleman explained that when he told his kids about the importance of a college education, they came back with: "Well Dad, you didn't graduate from college, you dropped out."

To this, Neeleman replied: "Okay, you go to college and if you find something better to do, and you think the time is right and you can make it happen, we'll discuss it. But in the meantime you're not going to sit around and do nothing, and you're not going to go work for someone else without a college education."

"I would be hypocritical if I told someone that they *need* a college education," Neeleman told us. "But I do value education. It teaches you to think analytically, but being someone who didn't graduate from college, I can't require that everybody does it. I really value what college does for people but, to a point. It keeps you kind of running on the same race track as everybody else."

While David Neeleman left college early, Wally Amos told us

that he didn't finish high school. He did, however, go back to get a General Equivalency Diploma (GED).

"I don't have a lot of *formal* education, but I think that education in the academic sense *is* important," Amos says. "Knowledge is important. You need to have access to it so you can use it at some point. I think that the thing that helped me most is that I had a belief in myself. I started Famous Amos with an educational background that some people might consider a handicap, with maybe even several handicaps. I was black, I didn't have a high school diploma, nor did I have experience in starting a retail store of any kind. Yet I moved forward and launched Famous Amos in five months. I later lost Famous Amos, but not because of my lack of education. I lost it because my ego got in the way. Education is important. There *are* some things that you actually do have to go to school to learn; otherwise, you're just not going to get them."

We asked Amos, if he was mentoring someone today, whether he would strongly recommend that he or she pursue higher education.

"It's no question," he replied. "I share this opinion with people all the time. I actually think it's *very* critical for them to get an education. There is another aspect of it that I think people sometimes overlook. Being a college graduate kind of puts you in a club. My daughter Sarah graduated from the University of Southern California, where they have one of the strongest alumni organizations of any school going. She can go to so many places and say that she graduated from USC—and chances are that someone there will be a USC alum. In that case, the fact that she is from USC will be a benefit. It's like being a member of a club where all the members support one another."

The first thing Gary Hirshberg said when we asked him if

higher education was important was that there is "No question." Hirshberg also told us that Stonyfield Farm provides tuition credit reimbursement and other incentives to employees.

"Education is especially important today when knowledge is so transient," he added. "My 12-year-old knows more about technology than I'm ever going to know. I'm a deep believer in being sure that folks know where they can go to learn to keep up. I'm a huge believer in writing skills and speaking skills. You can have all the knowledge in the earth but, if you can't communicate it effectively, then it's useless."

Ben Cohen sees education as having more value for a person looking for a job than for an entrepreneur. For him and Jerry Greenfield, the practical part of their education before starting Ben & Jerry's was a correspondence course in ice-cream making from Pennsylvania State University. As Ben puts it: "I dropped out of school and that limited my options in terms of working for somebody else, but it led me to starting my own business."

In support of Cohen's contention, it is interesting that about 15 percent of the people on the *Forbes 400* list of richest people have not finished college.

As with David Neeleman, David Oreck left college early. Like many entrepreneurs, he describes himself as being mostly self-taught. For him, it was a matter of World War II interrupting his education.

"I had started college when Pearl Harbor came along and I promptly enlisted in the U.S. Army Air Force," Oreck explained. "When I got out of the military, I was anxious to get a job, make a living, and get married. Many guys went back and completed their education, but I did not. Frankly, I feel that, with what I've done,

> "It's because they don't complain, they show up on time, their shoes are shined, they present themselves professionally, and they follow directions…"
>
> —David Oreck

I've gotten a better education than a lot of people who had the benefits of a formal education."

When we asked what he would recommend if he were advising a young person today, he said "I certainly wouldn't recommend doing what I did; it was the hard way."

He added that military experience, as much as higher education, is a strong plus in developing a person for the business world. He cites the fact that many companies are eager to hire management people who have been in the service. "It's because they don't complain, they show up on time, their shoes are shined, they present themselves professionally, and they follow directions," he said. "I think that every young person should serve two or three years in the military. I think that it would give him or her some direction, some focus in his or her life, and some appreciation of what this country stands for. From his or her own standpoint, he and she are learning something. I think that a kid who is 18 years old and going into college doesn't know a thing. If I were ever to go back to school, I would get a hell of a lot more out of it than I would have at 18. I think that it would be wonderful if a person had the benefit of two or three years in the military."

Oreck cited an example from his own experience: "Several years ago I hired a woman who had graduated from the U.S. Coast Guard Academy. She was out of the service and looking for a job. She didn't know anything about our business, or doing business, so I hired her at a very low salary. Today she's one of the top people in the company. She's damned good, and I have the highest regard for her. It was one of the best decisions I've ever made. So I would say, given a choice of people, with about equal qualifications, I would take the former military person every time."

> "The real entrepreneurs recognize their strengths and weaknesses and hire to their weaknesses."
> —Jeff Taylor

Business Tools

Having discussed education, we followed up by asking the entrepreneurs what tools they have used, what sorts of books they've read, and what they would recommend. In our experience, most business leaders have found personal and professional growth tools, as well as groups such as the Young Presidents' Organization and the Entrepreneurs' Organization, to be *highly* beneficial and facilitators of growth.

Jeff Taylor told us that he used coaches along the way, specifically around strategy. "I think that sometimes it's good to go to the outside to get some help with strategy," he explained. "Some people can hire people around them who are better than they are, and other people can't. I've always had good people. The real entrepreneurs recognize their strengths and weaknesses and hire to their weaknesses. I find that if you do a good job hiring, those people become your sounding board for building a good business."

We next asked Taylor to tell us about his reading habits. "I like books about adventure and about experiences," he said. "I find that they're incredibly stimulating because, as you are going through exhilarating moments in the book, you find that your brain is working on problems in your own current life as well. I typically prefer books such as *Into Thin Air: A Personal Account of the Mt. Everest Disaster* by Jon Krakauer, or Sebastian Junger's *The Perfect Storm: A True Story of Men Against the Sea*, or *In The Heart of The Sea* by Nathaniel Philbrick, as well as books about Lewis and Clark. I've also read business books such as *Who Moved My Cheese? An Amazing Way to Deal with Change in Your Work and in Your Life* by Dr. Spencer Johnson, and Malcolm Gladwell's *The Tipping Point: How Little Things Can Make a Big Difference.* I read tidbit books that give you pointers on how to be a better manager, but I usually don't read business books because I draw enough horsepower from my own business. If I read too much of that, I can't remember whether I have original ideas or whether I'm plagiarizing ideas from somewhere else."

"I'm not really a voracious reader," David Neeleman told us when we asked what books he reads. "I don't sit down and consume a book over a weekend. I couldn't possibly do that. I just really love watching other businesses and watching their practices. I think that I'm a good observer. I try to listen, and I try to surround myself with really good people."

David Oreck describes himself as an avid reader. "I read everything in terms of trade publications and things that are relevant, and I read other stuff too," he told us. "I'm busy from the time I get up to the time I go to sleep. I read everything I can that's current and certainly everything that is relevant from a business standpoint."

When we asked Andy Spade what sorts of personal or business growth tools he had used, and whether he uses a strategic coach to help with goal setting, he told us that, for the most part, he and Kate prefer private conversations with fellow entrepreneurs and with friends who are innovators and thinkers—much like the people we have included in this book.

"I talk to them about problems," he explained. "I talk to old friends in business and ask them what they think of an issue. We have taken media coaching, which is a tool to learn how to deal with things and people. I do a lot of teaching and lecturing at various colleges myself. For a number of years, I taught classes at various art schools on strategy and entrepreneurship. I've also engaged in dialogue with the professors at business schools. I'm always seeking information."

Spade added that he does read a lot of books. "Some are specifically business books, and some are fiction or art books that give me a lot of inspiration and teach me things. I draw from everywhere. I like marketing books. I read them all of the time."

We asked him whether he felt that there was anything missing from the books on marketing that he had read. "In our experience, they have shortcomings in that they are often written in 'business speak,'" he explained. "They are art directed to *look* like business books, and they are always in the business section. Business, we have felt, is a life-living thing, not a technical thing. Business books should have pictures, including photography, and not merely charts and graphs. Photography used in a really innovative way could take a piece of advice and somehow show it to the reader in an intelligent way. Anecdotes that show things that happen to people and that give you advice are really great."

Bobbi Brown has very well-defined ideas about how her personal tools are her business tools.

> "All I want to do is be a better person and, if I can be a good person, then I think I'll attract the right people. I believe that, if I do the right things, then everything will work out."
> —Wally Amos

"I have incredibly healthy eating habits—the best food from brown rice to great protein to healthy vegetables with no chemicals. I feel better that way," she told us. "People in my office eat whatever they want on their own, but when we have business meetings, sales meetings, and retailer meetings, people eat the way I eat. It has given me the most amazing confidence. The difference between me now and when I started my company is that I didn't have enough confidence to tell certain people—whether it was retailers, or partners—that things had to be done in a certain way that was right for me. I had a big turnaround in my company a few years ago when it started going flat. It was really scary. I told the higher-ups that they had a choice: Either let me do what I think is right, or I'm out. They said to go for it. We moved the company downtown, I got the president of my dreams and I took away the dress code. I made everything very 'Bobbi,' and ever since, things have never been better."

We found that everything about Bobbi is authentic. Authenticity builds brand equity, and this was certainly evident to the Estée Lauder Corporation when they acquired the brand in 1995, and kept Bobbi on board to manage and spearhead it.

When we asked Wally Amos what personal or professional growth vehicles he had used, he told us that there had been a time when he was going in for "all types of seminars."

"The things that I've always worked on are developing my life and my consciousness spiritually," he explained. "I don't need to go to business seminars because I'm not going to be the one to run the business. I'm a promoter, not a business person. I know how to promote. I know intuitively and instinctively what will work. That's my strength, so that's what I do."

When we asked him to elaborate on his interest in personal growth, he said: "All I want to do is be a better person and, if I can be a good person, then I think I'll attract the right people. I believe that if I do the right things, then everything will work out. In order to be a good person, it's important for me to have a good base spiritually, and to continue to work on that. My wife Christine and I give to those who are less fortunate than we are in terms of attitude and what not. It's so basic, I treat people the way I want to be treated. I don't go to seminars any more, although I give about 100 each year. Sharing my attitude and belief system with people, I'm just working on building a stronger foundation, and then all the other things will fall into place."

This level of authenticity helps a company or entrepreneur to connect viscerally and emotionally with its customers!

Side by side with personal and business growth tools in an entrepreneur's toolbox are marketing tools. When we asked David Neeleman what branding tools or marketing practices he credits for the success of JetBlue, the first thing he mentioned was "just creating word-of-mouth."

"It's a case of getting people aboard, dazzling them on a flight, and letting them spread the word," he smiled. "You look at our brand-new carpet, our leather seats, and the seat-back television screens, and you imagine customers realizing that they're getting all this for sixty-nine bucks! I think there was a disparity between

> "If there is no intention of going public or having broad ownership, then to give options or 'phantom stock' would be very cynical."
>
> —Jerry Baldwin

what people felt they were getting and the price they paid for it. The wider the disparity, the more buzz it creates. If you were able to buy a five-hundred-dollar Nikon camera for fifty bucks, you'd tell a hundred people about it. We were able to create a company where you get so much more value than the price that you pay. Meanwhile, our people are so much friendlier than you've experienced before. It created an enormous amount of buzz. I think that's what has made us most successful."

When we asked Andy Spade which marketing tools had been most effective in brand-building, his one-word answer was "Kate." Most of our other entrepreneurs credit public relations, community relations, cause marketing, sampling, and creative promotions with their successes.

Sharing Equity and Taking on Partners

For many entrepreneurs, parting with an equity share in something that is their brainchild can be a difficult thing to do. Nevertheless, most of those whom we interviewed for this book believe in giving equity and sharing the responsibility and the rewards of the company that they started. Many of the most authentic companies do not pay the highest salaries. People work there for many reasons. It might be because of the stance of management on a particular issue, because they enjoy the work, because employees are treated respectfully by management—or because they hope to one day own a share in the company they are helping to build.

Ben Cohen and Jerry Greenfield told us that they parted with little equity before their initial Vermont-only stock offering in 1984. "When we went public, we gave some stock to our employees and I felt great about it," Ben recalls. "I think down the line selling stock certainly created a major problem in that we were unable to keep the company independent." (In August 2000, Ben & Jerry's was acquired by the Dutch industrial giant, Unilever, which also then owned numerous other ice cream brands—from Good Humor to Breyers—in the United States.)

David Neeleman explained that JetBlue has stock options for managers, directors and vice presidents, pilots and technicians. "It's very, very important for what we do," he explained. "We have the most aggressive stock purchase plan allowed by IRS regulations. People can buy at a discount, and then they can lock in that stock price for two years. That's why we have such a high percentage of our people participating in the stock-purchase program. I think it's important to have people own a piece of the rock."

Like Neeleman, Jim Koch and Gary Hirshberg both believe in a stock plan for employees and both of them provided equity to employees from the beginning. When Koch's Boston Beer Company started as a private firm in 1984, employees were given "phantom stock," which follows the value of the company without having redeemable cash value. By definition, phantom stock provides a cash or stock bonus based on the value of a stated number of shares, to be paid out at the end of a specified period of time. When the company went public, the phantom stock converted to real stock and people who had been with Boston Beer for eight or nine years made half a million dollars or more.

Wally Amos told us that he believes a company has to give equity to key people: "I don't know what the formula is or how that works out. There are people who have been very instrumental in helping me launch my Chip and Cookie brand, and I want them to have ownership in a real way. I do think that people should have to buy their way into a situation, though. If you put your own money up, then you'll treat it differently than if someone gave it to you as a gift."

On the other hand, David Oreck was very emphatic that he does not believe in giving equity to key executives—although he did tell us that he would consider profit as an incentive and a creative form of compensation.

Jerry Baldwin told us that he believes in giving equity to people within an organization, but he added the caveat that "One has to be careful with private companies."

"You have to be careful about what you're doing—whether it's with partners or diluting equity," he said, elaborating on his thoughts about equity sharing. "*If* there is no intention of going public or having broad ownership, then to give options or 'phantom stock' would be very cynical. Today, everybody is going to go public and get rich, but you have to be clear on your objectives. Over the years we've had a lot of requests to share in ownership, but how are you going to do it?"

Pursuing this thought, we asked, if someone is ownership-minded *and* he or she is a solid player in the organization, how does one keep him or her interested if he or she doesn't own a piece of the business?

"Today, the options package is extremely important when you hire an executive," Baldwin agreed. "We *do* have options going down to at least the store-manager level, and it has gone deeper in the past."

Having said this, Baldwin went on to give us his thoughts on options expensing, the currently popular practice of accounting for the value of share options that were distributed as incentives to employees, within the profit and loss reporting of a listed business.

"I don't think options expensing is a very good idea. Personally I'd be interested to see how it comes out. Having to account for options on the profit-and-loss statement will have the effect in reducing them, when the thing we ought to be doing is expanding them. It was well before I figured this out, that I had an insight that the people who are doing well from gains in net worth—rather than cash in their pockets—were those who owned stock. When a company is starting out, stock is not really worth anything. In our case, we were always in debt up to our eyeballs, so the idea that the shares could actually be worth something was for later."

He continued with his thoughts on a practical way of using forms of equity as true compensation: "I understand that ownership is the most powerful thing, more than a bonus, and more than salary. When we were about the size where we could start to think about going public, and as soon as that course of action was set in motion, we started handing out options. But if you have a family business, or a closely held business, equity can't be a part of the deal. If you take polls of what people say, and I believe it's consistent with their behavior, for most people, salary is not the primary or secondary goal of the job. Money comes in fourth or fifth."

Some entrepreneurs part with shares later in the evolution of their companies, while others have silent backers from the inception.

"A lot of people have angel investors, but they have to ask themselves how much they are willing to give up," Andy Spade told us, discussing the initial bankrolling of the company that he

> **"It's good to go talk with people who have experience and ask them what they would watch out for."**
> **—Andy Spade**

and Kate started. "If the business takes off, the entrepreneur finds himself sitting on this huge business, but cursing the investor for the percentage that the entrepreneur does not own. At one point, Kate and I sat down and decided we wanted to leave the business because we were exhausted. We had enough cash to pay everybody, so we weren't going to go bankrupt. It would be very fair. We could pay off everyone we owed, pay ourselves, and just go back to our old jobs. We'd had a good run. It was fun, and we're done. Then someone asked if we knew how many people worked for us, and how many people left good jobs for this. We realized that we had to keep it going, so we decided to find a majority partner and give him or her an option to buy us out at a later time. There are so many things to think about, that you *don't* think about in the beginning. It's good to go talk with people who have experience and ask them what they would watch out for."

Creating an Exit Strategy

The business leaders interviewed for this book built authentic brands with loyal followings and significant *brand equity*. In so doing, they were appealing not only to consumers, but also to potential purchasers of their companies. As we have seen, Bobbi Brown sold her company to Estée Lauder, while Kate and Andy Spade sold the majority of theirs to Neiman Marcus. In both cases, of course, the brand equity was so great and so well-established that the founders were asked to remain as custodians of the brand. For this, they were well compensated with shares in their new corporate parent.

Though Bobbi Brown sold her company to cosmetics giant Estée Lauder in 1995, she still retains a great degree of control. "There are certain things in my business that I just won't let go of, even though the higher-ups think it's ridiculous," she explained. "From little things like naming my products—to the colors. They ask me why I don't hire someone to do this. It's because they're mine, my vision. But I now have a president who runs the company, and who is someone who totally believes in me and in my style of working."

Gary Hirshberg had an employee stock plan in place at Stonyfield Farm, but he had to modify his original program when French-based Group Danone (makers of Dannon Yogurt, among other products) purchased all non-employee owned shares of Stonyfield stock in December 2003.

"That was probably the hardest single decision when we went with Danone," Hirshberg said. "It wasn't that they don't believe in equity. People do get stock options as incentives in their company. But our complicated capital structure didn't really fit for them to buy into a continuation of our stock plan. So, what we did was enable any employees who wanted to remain stock-holders. They were, of course, welcome to keep their stock and many did, although some didn't. This was curious to me. We weren't allowed to do a new stock initiative, and that was sad to me. They have to have equity options for equity opportunities which give them a long-term stake. They have to have incentives, profit-sharing or some kind of bonus program that keeps them focused on short-term measurable performance. They also need open-book management. They have to know what's going on. I see zero benefits to keeping employees in the dark about financials. As a matter of fact,

> "Even though they say they're going to be an 'investment partner,' they're not going to get involved as a true partner would; they're not going to be living it everyday."
>
> —Andy Spade

reciprocally, I see enormous benefit in being sure that there is an opportunity, no less than twice annually, for everyone to look at what's going on."

In this way, Hirshberg is a practitioner of the business-administration technique known as Open-Book Management. It was originally developed by Jack Stack and his team at Springfield Remanufacturing Corporation (now SRC Holdings), and made popular by John Case in his 1995 book *Open-Book Management: The Coming Business Revolution*. As discussed in the previous chapter, and as implied in the name, the method involves giving employees access to all pertinent financial data—such as revenue, profit, and cost of goods—about the company in order that they will be able to make better workplace decisions. Stack is the author of *The Great Game of Business* and *A Stake in the Outcome: Building a Culture of Ownership for the Long-Term Success of Your Business*.

Kate and Andy Spade told us that they believe in giving equity and they have. "Kate and I founded the company in 1993, and we brought two good friends into the business the second year," he explained. "It was a bootstrap business. We agreed on a handshake to trade equity for employment. I believe, that if they are valuable people, they *deserve* it. Sharing equity helped us to do business without seeking outside financial backing. In my opinion, such financial backing comes from someone who won't actually work in the business. Even though they say they're going to be an 'investment partner,' they're not going to get involved as a true partner would; they're not going to be *living it* everyday. I don't think they'll understand the way someone in-house will understand. I'd rather have someone as a partner who *works*, than someone who doesn't. That's better for me. I give equity up to people who work for it."

On the subject of equity-sharing, Andy Spade speaks to those who might hesitate to give away something of their own, when he says: "Friends of mine have said that they'd never give up equity. If they've built it, they want to own 100 percent, but the right people can help you do better financially and make the job more fun. A 100-percent share of a $2 million company is obviously less than a 50-percent share of $100 million. Kate and I never wanted to carry the cross ourselves, so we had two other partners. We didn't lose out on our thirties because we shared the day in and day out. In 1998, when we sold a majority of the company to the Neiman Marcus Group, we kept a 44-percent share. If things work out, that 44 percent will be more valuable than 100 percent."

"We've taken risks, but they've been calculated risks," Andy continued, reflecting on the evolution of the business. "When we sold to Neiman Marcus, we knew there was a risk that they could walk in here on any given day, and say 'Hey guys, we don't like you anymore so we're taking over. Goodbye.' We thought about this, and decided that the only reason it would happen would be that we weren't doing it well. We looked at all of the sides and told ourselves that if they bought it for $30 million, and in three years it was worth $5 million, and they wanted to run the company, they'd be welcome to kick us out. I would do exactly the same thing. In five years it had sales over $100 million."

We have learned from these entrepreneurs and the companies with which we've worked over the years that authenticity creates brand equity. Often, even despite financial health and devastating challenges, we find the value exaggerated because of the intangibles these brands possess. In other words, if you can create a "sticky" brand—one that attracts attention and commands customer loyalty—utilizing the tools described in this book, you can create the ideal exit strategy. Our interviewees have clearly demonstrated this fact.

Letting Go

Hand in hand with sharing equity, is the issue of an entrepreneur's sharing authority and responsibility for decisions within a business that he or she has created. Because a big part of entrepreneurs' success is their own ideas, and the execution of their ideas, control is often an issue. Many entrepreneurs talk about letting go of certain things while never losing the overall control, and the fine line that lies between. We tried to get a feeling for whether these entrepreneurs make the really big decisions themselves or get a consensus before making decisions, or whether they make each division head accountable and give each one autonomy when it comes to decision-making.

Wally Amos told us that he feels decisions should be made by a combination of these three approaches.

"I think consensus is important, but everything can't be consensus," he says. "You can't wait for everyone's opinion to make a decision. If you do, then nothing would get done. I think you must gain the trust of the people who work with you, so that when you make a decision, they know that you didn't make it from your ego or for your benefit, but that you made it for their and the company's benefit also. Surely you can't rely on a committee to run a business, or a consensus to make decisions. That's why you hire good people and you have to trust them to do that and you've got to work with them. And that's why you hire good public relations counselors and outside advisors."

> **"When you start something yourself, and you do everything except sweep the floor, letting go is very difficult, but it's important to do so in the interest of continuity."**
> **—David Oreck**

David Oreck, meanwhile, comes down firmly on the side of letting the person at the top make all the big decisions, especially if he or she is the entrepreneur who founded the company.

"I think that when you run a company, it's somewhat of a dictatorship," Oreck told us. "You might listen to people, but businesses don't run well by consensus. I think that's nonsense. I think that, if you're a good manager, you listen carefully, you evaluate everything you that you can—then you make the decision. Clearly, it's a decision that everyone probably won't agree with, but you have to make that judgment. If you're right more times than wrong, you stay on the job. If you aren't, you get the hell out of the way. To me, the very idea of consensus management is nonsense."

Nevertheless, Oreck went on to say that, when you do let go of any aspect of management, you have to also pass along the management authority to do the job. "When you start something yourself, and you do everything except sweep the floor, letting go is very difficult, but it's important to do so in the interest of continuity. I find that very difficult, but I do it, and I keep my trap shut. But

> "I think there's a gift that's been given to entrepreneurs that they have deep down in their gut. They feel what's right."
>
> —David Neeleman

I'll venture an opinion that this is absolutely, positively, what you must do. You can't turn something over to someone and not give him or her the authority. It *is* very difficult to let go when you've done it all yourself. However, I do think that you can keep your influence over others without directly controlling them."

Jeff Taylor agrees that the buck should stop with the entrepreneur at the top. While he told us that he believes in giving equity to key executives, sharing the top decision-making role is "not my style."

He went on to say, "I see advantages in both ways of doing it. I'm envious of people who have a brother or couple of people they've done business with, but I think my style is to be the boss." As for management consensus, or making decisions by consensus of a management team, Taylor said "I think you need to know when to say this is my decision, and I'm going to make it now."

When we asked David Neeleman about the issue of entrepreneurial control, he told us that he feels it's natural to want to be able to make sure everybody has a say, but he quickly added, "There are some times when you just have to say 'This is the way it's going to be.' Ultimately I'm responsible, even if JetBlue is a public company and I don't own the majority of the shares. I think there's a gift that's been given to entrepreneurs that they have deep down in their gut. They *feel* what's right. You can pressure-test it against other people, but you just have to go with your gut and say, 'I have to do it.' You need to be able to just make a decision. Sometimes it's unpopular, but you have to trust your instincts. I don't do this very often, but there are times when I feel like I have to. It's an uncomfortable thing to do, but I think it's very, very important."

Regarding the day-to-day operational decisions, Neeleman said: "When you have a big company, you can't always be passing pronouncements down from higher up, because you may not always have the right answer, even when you may think you do. I feel that I'm pretty involved in the operations. I know a lot about it, and I can answer a lot of questions having to do with the operations. However, if I have an idea about how I want something to be done, I can't just say 'this is the way it is and that's it.' I have to pull in the people who are responsible in that particular area and say 'This is my idea and, having looked at what's going on, I think we need to change this, so what do *you* think?' If they don't think that my idea will work, they will tell me so and *explain* their reasoning. I think you need to be able to stay in touch and know what you're talking about, but you need to rely on your people and then hold them accountable. You also have to be sure you don't give them an impossible task or a structure where they can't succeed."

"I don't have a tough time letting go," Jim Koch told us. "While I could do virtually everything in the company, I realize that there is somebody, at least one person, and often many people, who can do it better than I can. Why should I waste my time when we have people who can do better than I can?"

Even though Andy and Kate Spade were generous about giving equity to attract people who can help the business grow, including the sale of the majority share to Neiman Marcus, they still make the big decisions.

> "People will be more invested in executing the decision if they've had a part in forming it, or at least if they had a chance to register their objections. However, if you vote on it, you can come up with pretty stupid results."
>
> —Jerry Baldwin

"It's always Kate and I who call the shots on the top end in terms of strategic decisions, the direction of the business, what we want to do, what we don't want to do, and what kind of company we want to be," he told us. "We have a president, a senior management team, and our other two partners, all of whom are involved in that process as well. In most cases, we all talk about it and come to a conclusion, but generally the voice comes from my wife and me. In the certain areas, it's more Kate, and in certain areas it's more I, but overall it's the two of us."

When we asked Andy what he and Kate do when the naysayers start chiming in as a decision is being made, he said: "That's part of the problem, but part of the solution at the same time. You just tell them we're going to make it work."

Bobbi Brown explained that letting go is not really a challenge when she has confidence in the management team that is making the decisions. "I let go when I know that the team is in place," she says. "I have several different departments, from product development to public relations, from marketing to creative and, of course, sales. My president oversees the numbers guys. I don't have to worry about those things that I'm not good at."

Like other entrepreneurs with whom we spoke, Bobbi gravitates toward making decisions herself on important questions that reach her desk. "Most of the time, my decisions are instant," she explains. "One of the things that most people will say about me is that I am really clear about what I want probably 80 percent of the time. In the other 20 percent, when I'm not sure, I'm really open to learn something. Once I let my teenage boys pick the models for a campaign because all the books happened to be at our house. You know, I agreed with them. If I hadn't, I would have overruled them. Even if I'm really firm on a decision, I'll change my mind if there's a good reason—such as we can't afford it or we can't do it in time. I'm not difficult that way."

The importance of fast decision-making is discussed in Malcolm Gladwell's book *Blink: The Power of Thinking Without Thinking*. It is his belief that quick decisions, far from being erratic, are actually quite solid and authentic. As Gladwell describes it, rapid cognition, the kind of thinking that happens in a blink of an eye, can actually result in sound judgment: "When you meet someone for the first time, or walk into a house you are thinking of buying, or read the first few sentences of a book, your mind takes about two seconds to jump to a series of conclusions. Well, *Blink* is a book about those two seconds, because I think those instant conclusions that we reach are really powerful and really important and, occasionally, really good... Intuition strikes me as a concept we use to describe emotional reactions, gut feelings—thoughts and impressions that don't seem entirely rational. But I think that what goes on in that first two seconds is perfectly rational. It's thinking—it's just thinking that moves a little faster and operates a little more mysteriously than the kind of deliberate, conscious decision-making that we usually associate with 'thinking.'"

On the issue of decision-making, Jerry Baldwin told us that he does not believe in decision-making by consensus, but that executives should have input on the issue as the decision is being made.

"I believe that everyone should have input into this decision, so that, as much as possible, he or she will 'own' the decisions," he said. "People will be more invested in executing the decision if they've had a part in forming it, or at least if they had a chance to register their objections. However, if you vote on it, you can come up with pretty stupid results."

When we asked him whether letting go presented a challenge, he told us that in the early years, he thought of himself as "controlling," but over time, letting go was less of a challenge.

"I think the most important thing to develop in maturing is one's own reinforcement," he explained. "Few people realize that the person you have to convince that you are successful is the person you look at in the mirror every morning. You have to convince yourself. You don't have to convince anybody else. In the end, you have to say 'Good job!' to yourself, because, especially if you're running the company, not too many other people are going to tell you."

Macro-Managing—Not Micro-Managing

For many entrepreneurs, getting a perspective often means getting away. We've all been in that position of becoming so immersed in minutiae that we lose sight of the big picture. The old and overworked adage of "not being able to see the forest for the trees" comes to mind. Michael Gerber, the author of *The E-Myth Revisited: Why Most Small Businesses Don't Work and What to Do About It*, recommends getting away from the office to keep things in perspective. As he puts it, "instead of working *in* your business, work *on* your business."

It is generally assumed that most people want to start their own business so they can work for themselves, rather than for someone else. In a recent interview with *Management Consulting News*, Gerber was asked about the motive of achieving some degree of freedom being behind the decision by entrepreneurs to start their businesses.

> "Everybody writes books on how to start a business. But nobody writes about how to get out."
>
> —Andy Spade

"They want to be their own boss and make their own choices and decisions," Gerber said. "That's admirable, and it seems like it would liberate you to do what you love without the interference of a boss. Unfortunately, it often makes your situation worse. You have that enormously positive expectation that you'll be free, and then you realize that you are in a worse prison than before because it's one of your own making.

"That sounds terribly tragic and depressing, and it's all of that and more. Once you are free of the boss and become self-employed, you're caught in this vicious cycle—can't get out of it, can't get out of it. Now I'm doing what I believed I would love to do and I'm more consumed than ever, and doing many more jobs than I did in the past."

Andy Spade told us of an experience that directly echoed Gerber's comments: "I had a friend who said he wanted to get out of working in a company and have his own restaurant. He didn't realize that his lifestyle was soon to become one of working until 2:00 a.m. every night overseeing the business. He was miserable. He told me that he felt trapped. A business isn't always freedom. Think it through before you jump in."

> **"If you want a retail store, don't open it too close to your home, because you'll get obsessive about it—and lose sight of the bigger picture."**
>
> **—Andy Spade**

Gerber went on to explain, "The essence of a business plan that always works is that it's not first and primarily about creating a business. Instead, it's about what you want. The question you have to ask yourself is, 'What do I want?' If that's not driving it, then it becomes an empty process."

Spade's advice on the subject is simple: "Strategize your *life* before you strategize your business. I think it is important to know how you want to live, and what you want to do, because your life and your business become *one* if you are starting your own company. Everybody writes books on how to start a business," he mused, reflecting on the issue of exit strategies, "but nobody writes about how to get *out*. I have another friend who has businesses that no one wants to buy. He can't sell them. He has too much invested. He really wants to move to the country, so he left another well-paying job to take a risk with a business model that was more salable."

Spade continued, explaining what he tells people who come to him for advice as they are thinking about starting their own company. "You really need to look at it," he tells them. "You need to ask yourself, if I do X, Y and Z, where I will be three years from now, or five years from now? It could be a trap. A lot of people prove you wrong but it is really hard. It is really, really hard, but I will always say *do it*. I would almost never say don't do it."

He went on to explain how some entrepreneurs become trapped by their commitments to the investors—not to mention employees—who made their business possible in the first place.

Spade told us that he has little trouble distancing himself from operational issues and focusing on what he really wants, but that Kate has a hard time letting go. He told us that she overcomes the entrepreneurial control factor by "getting away from the office, getting out of town, getting perspective, and looking at other things. You have to realize that there are so many other things going on in the world, and this is so unimportant in the scheme of things."

From experience, Spade says, "If you want a retail store, don't open it close to your home, because you'll get obsessive about it —and lose the bigger picture. Kate and I do. We work off-site quite a bit when we're traveling. Being away for a month at a time, we actually get a lot of work done. In fact, that's when we get *most* of the work done. Kate has worked from the house a lot, and this is actually more productive for us. I think that it's an important way to be able to let go and control your emotions—and keep off business."

Bobbi Brown agrees with the Spades that stepping back is a good way of keeping things in perspective. As she told us: "Being out of the office a couple of days a week, stepping back and thinking about things, is definitely mind-clearing."

As Michael Gerber told *Management Consulting News*, the one piece of advice that he'd give an entrepreneur is to "go into the dreaming room continuously, passionately, with conviction, and not to be in a rush to know. The dreaming room is the place where not knowing happens. Our problem is we want to get to knowing too fast, and that knowledge almost always comes from the past. We live in the past with what we've learned, and that becomes our limited arsenal for shaping our future, which is unknown.

You don't go to the dreaming room to discover how; you go to learn about the form and shape of what. And you need to take that slowly. Because to the degree you jump into how, you're immediately reverting to the past."

Leaving a Legacy

The dictionary defines "legacy" as *something bequeathed or established for future generations*. The conversations that we had with these entrepreneurs regarding their own legacies dovetail nicely into this chapter that contains lessons from their experience and their successes.

We were just flies on the wall when Ben Cohen and Jerry Greenfield were discussing between themselves the importance and the legacy of the "Ben & Jerry's" brand.

"We've got immortality," Ben told his partner.

"Yeah, but who associates KFC with the Colonel?" Jerry asked, referencing the Kentucky Fried Chicken brand and its founder, Colonel Harland Sanders. "I don't think anybody does. It's not even Kentucky Fried Chicken anymore. Now it's just 'KFC,' because they don't want to use the word 'fried.' The founder's legacy with the brand lasts for some years, and then you're done."

"What do you think is going to help the legacy if you are not going to be remembered by the consumers of tomorrow?" we asked. "What's going to help keep the brand strong, and the message authentic?"

"What's *currently* being done," Ben replied, "is that the company is continuing to support the brand both in terms of finding new and innovative ways to solve social problems, and in making better and better and more innovative flavors of ice cream."

We then asked Ben and Jerry what they would give as advice to someone who was starting a business, or to someone who wanted to grow an existing business.

"I would suggest to somebody that he or she do something that they love," Jerry said, underscoring the heart and soul of the idea of authenticity. "You should do what you are passionate about, because there are always times or difficult periods when things are not going right. It really helps if you are doing something you love instead of something that you are just spending a bunch of money on. You can become very discouraged if you're not involved in something *genuine*, something that you believe in, and are committed to."

> "It really helps if you are doing something you love instead of something that you are just spending a bunch of money on. You can become very discouraged if you're not involved in something *genuine*, something that you believe in, and are committed to."
>
> —Jerry Greenfield

In looking at the legacy of the Kate Spade brand now that it is part of Neiman Marcus, Andy Spade told us: "We built a great foundation for the brand. Instinct and formal research show that the brand has a great reputation. Because of this reputation, consumers will accept that the brand can expand beyond the basic product line and do other things. The consumers give the brand a lot of credit for doing *authentic* and creative things outside of the typical accessory business model, which is good. For example, we have moved into home products, even music. I don't know where it will go, but I hope that it will continue to be managed by people who will utilize the values of the name for the better. If it's with smart, creative people, I think that they'll do well, as Chanel has. We have a great *story* to tell."

For the people who will manage the Kate Spade brand in the future, Kate and Andy have written a brand book for the business.

"It's like a guide," Andy explained. "They can follow it or not. We hope that they do. We put much value on our personal legacy, so we hope that people respect the ideas and values on which the business was formed."

When bequeathing advice for later generations, David Neeleman said that he would counsel younger entrepreneurs to "Treat your people right and make sure that, if you're building a service business, you don't build it on the backs of your people. Sometimes when you're starting out, you want to be cheap and you want to cut corners. *Don't do it.* That's the big lesson that I've learned."

Monster's founder Jeff Taylor, meanwhile, had three well-considered pieces of advice:

1. "First of all, Woody Allen said that '80 percent of life is just showing up', which many people don't do. The suggestion is to show up, and that could be anywhere from going to a networking meeting to getting out of bed an hour earlier to go work out, and showing up at the treadmill. Showing up has been a key factor for me."

2. "The second thing is, if you coast, you coast only one way and that's downhill. The only one who knows you're coasting in the beginning is *you*. A lot of times I think you can catch yourself before anyone else would ever know, and begin to climb and claw and work back to your successes. If you wait too long, then other

people recognize that you are coasting. By then, a lot of times, it's too late."

3. "The third thing is that the shortest distance between two points is—something we learn in the fourth grade—a straight line. However, the reality is that we're really brainwashed about this. Even today, most people are still trying to figure out how to work the straight line, but life doesn't work that way. Life is a pretty bent and messed-up line that somehow gets from the beginning to the end. I think that, if you can recognize this fact, a lot of times you can embrace an alternative strategy. I found out you will often really flourish more in the alternative, than in following what you may have thought you were *supposed* to do. I've worked a lot of my life with this idea, rather than thinking of a straight line as the shortest distance between two points. Make this a big idea."

Final Thoughts

Nearly 20 years ago, when I finished college, my brother-in-law Andy Bluestone generously introduced me to a man who was looking for a successor to run the transportation company that he had started in his mid-30s. It was a flourishing business and he was looking for the right person to lead his company into the future. While it was not a fit for me, I learned a great deal about him and about what made his business a success.

During the seven hours we spent together, he asked me about my philanthropic activities, my beliefs, and what I thought of others. He asked me to tell him specifically about past employers and about people whom I had managed.

Although he did not verbalize it in so many words, he had just shared with me his recipe for success. He had given me an insight into what enabled him to stay afloat even when his competitors had gone under due to uncontrollable factors such as industry volatility, fuel prices, and unionization. What I learned from this time with him was *what he stood for*—treating people with dignity, service and respect, and anticipating industry and economic shifts to prepare for the future.

His enduring focus on the customer, his restless desire for improvement, his conviction for giving, and his self-discipline were the things that set him apart from the competition. As you can see, all of these traits point to *authenticity*.

It is my belief, and that of these prominent business leaders with whom we spoke when writing this book, that the focus belongs on the customer. Today's consumers or business associates demand more, and they demand that we speak *to their intelligence*. Today's consumers are savvy. They understand that they have many options when it comes to products and services. If we deliver our products or services with authenticity, it is possible to start from nothing and grow to national acclaim. If we deliver exceptional quality, and if we deliver our product or service with exceptional thoughtfulness, the possibilities are limitless.

About the author:

Christopher Rosica
CEO, Rosica Strategic Public Relations
Author, The Authentic Brand

Christopher Rosica, CEO of Rosica Strategic Public Relations, is a recognized public relations and marketing expert, speaker, and author. He is passionate about entrepreneurship and helping businesses grow, adapt to change, outpace the competition, and improve internal and external communications. Rosica's national PR firm serves a variety of industries and specializes in media relations, message development, cause-related marketing, crisis communications/planning, and online marketing as a means of building brand awareness. An authority on cause marketing, Rosica also authored *The Cause Marketing Handbook: How Doing Good Means Doing Well* (Noble Press), which details the process and effects of incorporating cause marketing into a company's business and promotional agenda. He is a frequent keynote speaker, media trainer, and public speaking coach who teaches CEOs, salespeople, corporate and nonprofit executives, and college students. Rosica has lectured at Fordham, Seton Hall and PACE universities and numerous other colleges and universities in the NY metro area. As part of a symposium for the Young Presidents' Organization (YPO) and the Entrepreneurs' Organization (EO), Rosica received high accolades for his interview with renowned CEO Jack Welch. Rosica is past president of New York's Young Entrepreneurs' Organization (YEO), chairs the public relations committee for EO Global, and serves on several nonprofit boards, including Boys & Girls Clubs in New Jersey. In 2006, he completed the "Birthing of Giants," an exclusive three-year course on entrepreneurship at MIT sponsored by EO in conjunction with Inc. Magazine and the MIT Enterprise Forum. He recently completed the Leadership New Jersey curriculum, which connects the state's corporate, governmental and nonprofit leaders to affect positive change. Rosica is a graduate of Florida International and Johnson & Wales Universities and lives in New Jersey with his wife, Wendy, daughter, and son.